OZZZY AND BLACK SABBATH

WHAT EVIL LURKS

JOEL McIVER

chartwell
books

Quarto

Text © 2016 by Joel McIver

This edition published in 2022 by Chartwell Books,
an imprint of The Quarto Group
142 West 36th Street, 4th Floor
New York, NY 10018 USA
 T (212) 779-4972 F (212) 779-6058
www.Quarto.com

First published in the United States of America in 2016 by
Race Point Publishing, an imprint of
Quarto Publishing Group USA Inc.
142 West 36th Street, 4th Floor
New York, NY 10018 USA
www.Quarto.com

Every effort has been made to ensure that credits accurately comply with
information supplied.

We apologize for any inaccuracies that may have occurred and will resolve
inaccurate or missing information in a subsequent reprinting of the book.

10 9 8 7 6 5 4 3 2 1

ISBN: 978-0-7858-4369-6

Library of Congress Cataloging-in-Publication Data is available

Editorial Director: Jeannine Dillon
Managing Editor: Erin Canning
Project Editor: Jason Chappell
Art Director: Merideth Harte
Interior Design: Renato Stanisic
Cover Images: Sam Dunn

Printed in China

THIS BOOK IS DEDICATED TO THE LATE

IAN "LEMMY" KILMISTER,

WHOM I MET MANY TIMES AND GREATLY ADMIRED

CONTENTS

FOREWORD
BY ROBB FLYNN

It all started with a lyric.

"Make a joke and I will sigh, and you will laugh and I will cry / Happiness I cannot feel and love to me is so unreal."

It hit me like a ton of bricks. I'd never heard anything so depressing and dark in music. Up until then, music was uplifting, for the most part. If it was dark, it was usually "My baby left me," but this . . . ? Wow. I related to it in a way I cannot quite put into words.

It certainly didn't hurt that I was stoned out of my mind for the first time in my life. Having cut school with some buddies to smoke weed and listen to records, I wasn't prepared for the music my buddy Elvis— yes, that was his real name—played. As I sat there staring at the inner gatefold of *We*

Sold Our Souls for Rock 'n' Roll, gazing at the empty-eyed girl lying in a coffin with a chrome cross lying across her breast, I didn't know what the hell to think of this Black Sabbath band, but it scared the shit out of me—and I convinced myself that I would burn in hell for the rest of my life if I continued to listen to it.

Then my friend played "Iron Man"—and that was it.

"Turn it off!" I blurted. "This is freaking me out!"

Black Sabbath scared me so much I didn't want to listen to it any more.

Three days later, we cut school again. Elvis raided his dad's weed stash again, and we got high as kites—but this time, I had to hear Black Sabbath again. In those three

OPPOSITE: *Robb Flynn of Machine Head plays at Lucky Strike Live on January 22, 2016, in Hollywood, California.*

days I could not get that lyric out of my head, or the ridiculously catchy song that the lyric came from.

"Dude, put on that Black Sabbath again," I said.

This time, I was mesmerized. Evil, sinister, otherworldly, and impossibly heavy—I had never heard music like it. It blew me away, and from that point on I jumped headfirst down the rabbit hole.

I went about collecting every Sabbath album I could find. I searched out the rare US version with "Evil Woman" on it, and the semi-official bootleg *Live at Last*, where Ozzy fucked up most of the lyrics, but who cared! By the time I got to *Master of Reality*, that was it. They had me . . . forever. Songs about evil women, weed, mushrooms, cocaine, Satan, war, wanting to see the Pope at the end of a rope—I couldn't get enough.

Much is made about the satanic aspect of Black Sabbath, and I loved that side of them, but for me I was always struck by the protest/"fuck you" side of the band. An anti-war song like "War Pigs," written at the height of the Vietnam War, at a time when very serious repercussions could come to you for saying such things, was inspirational to me. Then there was "Hand of Doom," with its warning about heroin use, the questioning of authority, of religion, of the status quo . . . these guys became heroes to me. Hell, a teenage Robb Flynn even wrote them a letter imploring them to get back together and play my town— and if they did, I would proudly display a sign asking them to play "Sweet Leaf."

I've been fortunate enough to tour with Black Sabbath twice, and they were the real deal. Terrifyingly heavy, beautiful, magical, Sabbath are and always will be the greatest band of all time.

ROBB FLYNN, MACHINE HEAD
2016

INTRODUCTION

Black Sabbath, in any of its incarnations across its forty-seven-year career to date, is a force of nature. Inventing heavy metal and doom metal at a stroke, thrilling the wise with epic fantasy lyrics, and scaring the weak-witted with Satanic flirtations, Sabbath has done it all. That includes every high (commercial and substance-derived), low, and plateau imaginable, including periods of total unfashionability and others of godlike regard.

The band's final studio album, *13*, was a global hit, and the immense farewell tour that concluded in 2016 was a true colossus. Telling this band's story

ABOVE: *Photographs of (from left) Ozzy Osbourne, Bill Ward, Tony Iommi, and Geezer Butler from 1970.*

has been a privilege for me.

I've been talking to musicians for almost twenty years, and musos of the rock and metal persuasion tend to like Black Sabbath's music, so I've had no shortage of material to draw on. Interviews personally conducted by me over the last few years include chats with Ozzy, Tony, Geezer, and Bill themselves, plus sometime Sabbath alumni Glenn Hughes, Ian Gillan, Ronnie James Dio, Bob Daisley, Dave Spitz, and Tony Martin. Sabbath's first manager, Jim Simpson, provided plenty of illuminating insights, too.

Other musical luminaries who shared their opinions about Sabbath with me include Ritchie Blackmore, Bobby Rondinelli, Leo Lyons (Ten Years After), Tom Araya and Kerry King (Slayer), John Lydon, Ian "Lemmy" Kilmister, King Diamond, Nikki Sixx (Mötley Crüe), Bill Gould (Faith No More), Yngwie J. Malmsteen, Dave Mustaine (Megadeth), Geddy Lee (Rush), Zakk Wylde (Black Label Society), Paul Allender (Cradle of Filth), the late "Dimebag" Darrell Abbott (Pantera/Damageplan), Ice-T, Joey Jordison and Mick Thomson (Slipknot), Bobby

Ellsworth (Overkill), Jeff Becerra (Possessed), Conrad Lant and Jeff Dunn (Venom), John Bush (Armored Saint, Anthrax), Katon W. DePena (Hirax), Mikael Akerfeldt (Opeth), Phil Fasciana (Malevolent Creation), Sean Harris (Diamond Head), and Rob Halford (Judas Priest). Quite a stellar gathering, I'm sure you'll agree. These people give a truly widescreen perspective to the whole Sabbath story—and one that this most august of metal bands deserves.

This book accompanies Black Sabbath's farewell with a look back at a frankly insane career. Cheers to Ozzy, Tony, Geezer, and Bill: you really couldn't make this story up.

JOEL McIVER

OPPOSITE: *Black Sabbath photografhed in a giant shell in Long Beach in September, 1975.*

WHAT EVIL LURKS

1948–1969

John Michael Osbourne, born on December 3, 1948, and raised in the home of his parents Jack and Lillian at 14 Lodge Road in Aston, a bombed-out suburb of Birmingham, England, should by rights have spent forty-five years working in a factory before dying in his sixties. That was the career path laid down by tradition for men of his era and demographic. Instead, Ozzy—as we might as well refer to him from now on—became one of the world's most recognizable rock stars. What were the chances?

"Low" is the answer. His parents both worked in the automobile industry, with his dad on night shifts and his mum working at the Lucas company in its wiring plant. Aston had taken a beating during World War II, only four years before, and the poverty of the area

OPPOSITE: Ozzy photographed in August 1969 as a member of the band Earth, at Hamburg's Star-Club.
ABOVE: Bull Ring Centre, a brutalist redevelopment project in 1960s Birmingham.

was easily visible. Most of Aston's working population was confined to living conditions that would seem primitive to most observers in the pampered modern age in which you and I live. Ozzy, his brothers Paul and Tony, his sisters Jean, Iris, and Gillian, and their parents lived in typically cramped style.

Another local family, the Wards, lived on Witton Lodge Road. Their son William was born seven months before Ozzy, on May 5, 1948. Ward once described Aston as a no-frills place where violence was the order of the day; he witnessed stabbings and saw men coming out of pubs only to drop dead before his eyes. Vagrants abounded in the grim years of postwar shock, although he felt that Aston had a sort of beauty at the same time. For him, and for Ozzy, it was home.

As with any depressed urban area—and especially at this point in history—career options were limited, so a common option for young men who couldn't find work in a factory was to enter the army. The Butler family, whose youngest son Terence Michael Joseph was born on July 17, 1949, sent two other sons to the armed forces; the boys returned home periodically, having struck up friendships with soldiers from London. As a result, they had acquired the word "geezer"—synonymous with "guy" or "dude" in American English—and the term found its way into young Terence's vocabulary. The effect was that he gained the nickname himself, and thus "Geezer Butler" was born.

None of these three youths were exactly academic geniuses, although they all had an innate intelligence. Ozzy, who attended the King Edward VI Grammar School on Aston's Frederick Road, later described his school persona as "the original clown." Although he acted the buffoon to amuse his classmates, there was a darker side to his personality. At the tender age of fourteen, he attempted to hang himself. Hanging his mother's washing line over a bar that extended above head height across an alleyway between houses, Ozzy made a noose, placed it over his head, and climbed a chair. Making sure to hold tight to the rope—he wasn't seriously suicidal, it seemed—he jumped off the chair. His father caught him in the act, released his son from

LEFT: *Bill Ward photographed in August 1969 as a member of the band Earth, at Hamburg's Star-Club.*

certain death, and then beat him. Presumably that made a kind of sense.

Ozzy's school education included some pretty eye-opening incidents. On one occasion, he reportedly attacked one of his teachers with an iron bar (the teacher was subsequently fired for picking on him), and he got into occasional scrapes with an impassive but quick-fisted kid nine months his senior.

"Tony Iommi used to bully me all the time when I was at school," Ozzy later complained, as well he might—his adversary was a tough individual with the brawn to back up his temper. "It was always Tony who used to be the badass guy, going round beating

Geezer Butler (left) and Tony Iommi (below), members of the band Earth, photographed at Hamburg's Star-Club in August 1969.

everybody up," Geezer recalled. "He's totally mellowed out now, though."

Frank Anthony Iommi was born on February 19, 1948, and lived on Park Lane in Aston. "Aston was tough," he told me, "it really was—but it depends what you compare it to. We had stabbings and gangs, although there weren't any shootings then. It kept you on your toes, and you couldn't relax—you had to be careful wherever you went, because if you weren't a member of a particular gang, you were against them, and it was very awkward. . . . Ozzy was a year younger than me [at school], and he had a couple of mates who me and my friends didn't always get on with. Still, it was a long time ago. At our school you had to be like that or you got beaten up."

JOINING THE ARMY

Despite his dislike of school, Ozzy found some solace as a performer in hokey pseudo-operatic productions of old stage standards such as *H.M.S. Pinafore*, *The Mikado*, and *The Pirates of Penzance*. But this didn't deter him from leaving school at the first possible opportunity, which in England then was the age of fifteen.

The adult world of work was hardly welcoming. Ozzy's first job was as a toolmaker's apprentice, and he cut off the end of his thumb on the very first day. Having had the missing chunk sewed back on, he moved through a succession of desperate jobs, including killing livestock in an abattoir. Another particularly terrible job

was assembling car horns in a factory, where he felt his sanity slowly giving way under the noisy conditions.

In 1965, in an attempt to escape the factories, Ozzy tried to join the army. "I was seventeen and pissed off," he told the writer Sylvie Simmons. "I wanted to see the world and shoot as many people as possible—which is not much different from being in a band these days—the rap world, anyway. How far did I get? About three feet across the fucking front door. They just told me to fuck off. He said, 'We want subjects, not objects.' I had long hair, a water tap on a string around my neck for jewelry, I was wearing a pajama shirt for a jacket, my arse was hanging out, and I hadn't had a bath for months. And my dad would say, 'You've got to learn a trade'—he was a toolmaker. I thought joining the army would please him."

The tedium was briefly interrupted in 1966 by a stint in prison for breaking and entering, which Ozzy had messed up gloriously. He was an incompetent burglar at best, on one occasion wearing fingerless gloves while attempting to steal goods from a local clothes store called Sarah Clarke. After turning down

BELOW: *Birmingham's Winson Green Prison, where Ozzy spent some time in 1966.*

the offer of paying a £25 fine—a hefty sum in those days, equating to around $70 at the time—he served six weeks of a three-month jail term in Birmingham's Winson Green Prison, a forbidding Victorian institution built in 1849. A second spell in prison followed when Ozzy chose, in his infinite wisdom, to punch a policeman squarely in the face. While inside, he at least partially alleviated the daily boredom by tattooing "O-Z-Z-Y" across his left knuckles with a sewing needle.

Having served these two prison sentences, it seemed fairly obvious to even the most charitable observer that Ozzy's career was headed in one of two directions: toward either the gutter or the graveyard. The army wouldn't have him, he couldn't tolerate factory life, and

ABOVE: *While in prison in 1966, Ozzy tattooed his name across his left knuckles with a sewing needle.*

he was too much of a tearaway to settle down. Music was his only solace, just as it was for Iommi, Butler, and Ward—three boys with fewer antisocial tendencies than Ozzy, but whose career outlooks were just as poor.

Many years later, in unimaginably different circumstances, Ozzy told the author of this book what the Beatles meant to him. "They were the only band to start off like New Kids on the Block and end up like Pink Floyd," he mused. "I don't think there's any other band who have done that. People ask me how many albums I've got left and I say, 'I haven't done my *Sgt. Pepper* yet.' That album was fucking phenomenal."

It was an exciting time to be into pop music, or "beat," as it was then known. When the Beatles released "Love Me Do" in October 1962, the Aston foursome were aged between thirteen and fourteen—the perfect age to be smitten by the music bug. Ward had started learning to play the drums as a preteen. "I just wanted to be a musician: any idea of making a living out of it was an afterthought," he later told me. "We were lucky if we could look six months ahead. That was where we were: we had a day, and we'd do what we needed to do to fill that day, and then we'd do it again when the next day arrived. I don't think any of us had any long-term visions of how we were going to be or what we were going to do. There was no control as far as anticipation of the future went."

IN WITH THE IN CROWD

Tony Iommi, meanwhile, was pouring his efforts into learning the guitar. By the age of fifteen, he'd made rapid progress, knuckling down to the business of learning chords with the grim determination that had made him so feared in the schoolyard. In 1963, he joined a band called the Pursuers, in which he played a cheap guitar called a Watkins Rapier. "It was very cheap!" he told me. "I was attracted to it because it was left-handed—and in those days you didn't really get lefties. Jesus, did I really buy it over fifty years ago?"

His next gigs came with two short-lived acts called the In Crowd and the Birds and the Bees. These didn't last long, although a slightly more reliable act called the Rockin' Chevrolets—also featuring Neil Cressin (vocals), Alan Meredith (guitar), Dave Whaddley (bass), and Pat Pegg (drums)—became known locally for its live act. The band's weekly appearances at the Bolton Pub in Small Heath would include renditions of instrumentals by groups such as the Shadows and the Dakotas, during which Iommi's skills on his instrument impressed onlookers—even though he was still in his mid-teens.

In 1965, the Rockin' Chevrolets were offered gigs in West Germany, where a long line of British bands, beginning with the Beatles, would go on to build a reputation for world-class gigs. Iommi decided it was time to hand in his notice at the sheet-metal factory where he worked. On his very last day, he arrived at work ready to operate his heavy-duty machine press for the final time.

"It's funny, really," he laughed, when I asked him about what happened next. "On the day it happened, I was actually leaving that job to go and be a guitarist full-time—it's mad when you think about it."

As Iommi worked the machine, counting down the hours before European stardom could begin, his hand suddenly became trapped inside it. "I got the middle fingers on my right hand caught in it," he recalled, "and, without thinking, I pulled them out quickly. The weight on them was so great that [the ends] of those fingers stayed behind—down to the first joint on the middle finger, and most of the way down to the joint on the ring finger."

Hospital doctors stopped the bleeding and even managed to save Iommi's fingernails.

As he recalled, the nails were broken off and then surgically re-implanted. However, it took weeks for the fingers to heal, and even then they never completely regained their dexterity. As he told me, "To this day it hasn't really healed: there's only a couple of layers of skin over the ends of the bone, and if I bend those fingers, they still hurt. Believe me, I've looked into every conceivable way of getting them repaired surgically. They want to pull the skin forward from the rest of the finger to make a bigger covering at the fingertip, but I really don't want to do that."

One of the obvious problems now posed to Iommi by the injury to his right hand—perhaps luckily for him, as a left-hander, it was not the hand he used most in day-to-day life—was how to hold down the guitar strings with two fingertips missing. The damage might not have been important had it occurred to his picking hand, but any guitarist will tell you that the fretting fingertips need to have calluses on them if the instrument is to be played effectively. "I had to work really hard to get 'round it," he said. "I had to play more simply: there were certain chords I couldn't play and some extensions I couldn't do. I had to think of ways of playing that were effective but still possible for me."

Fortunately for Iommi—and for the entire future of heavy metal—he was inspired by the gypsy-jazz guitarist Django Reinhardt, who had died in 1953. Having developed a way of playing his instrument without using the third and fourth fingers on his fretting hand,

ABOVE: *Django Reinhardt developed a way of playing an instrument without using the third or fourth fingers on his fretting hand, inspiring Tony Iommi after his accident.*

which had been irreparably damaged in a fire, Reinhardt became known as a fast and fluent guitarist. Iommi noted this and eventually hit on the strategy of attaching home-made clips to his injured fingertips to reduce the pain of holding down a string.

He explained, "I melted down a Fairy Liquid [detergent] bottle, made a couple of blobs of the plastic, and then sat there with a hot soldering iron and melted holes in them so they'd fit on the tips of my injured fingers, kind of like thimbles. When I got the caps to fit comfortably, I ended up with these big balls on the ends of my fingers, so I then proceeded to file them down with sandpaper until they were approximately the size of normal fingertips."

This was no easy task, he added. "It took me quite a while to get them exactly right, because they couldn't be too heavy or thick, but they had to be strong enough so they didn't hurt the ends of my fingers when I used them. When I'd sculpted my 'thimbles' to the right size and tested them, I realized that the ends weren't gripping the strings, so I cut up a piece of leather and fixed pieces to the ends of them. I then spent ages rubbing the leather pads so they'd get shiny and absorb some oils, and would help me grip the strings better. I filed down the edges so they wouldn't catch on anything—and it worked!

"Once I'd done this, it took me quite a while to get used to bending and shaking the strings with those two fingers, because I obviously couldn't feel anything. It was even difficult to know where my fingers were and where they were going, [but] it was just a matter of practicing and persevering with it, using my ears to compensate for my lost tactile sense."

A couple of years down the line, Iommi further improved his technique by tuning his guitar down from standard E tuning to E-flat, reducing the string tension and making it easier to fret the notes. The consequence of this was that the chords he played were lower in pitch and what we would now call "heavier," although in 1965 this term was pretty meaningless.

THE RARE BREED

While all this was going on, drummer Bill Ward was looking for a band. Having already persuaded a singer, Chris Smith, and a bassist, Neil Marshall, to join him, he asked Iommi—now playing his guitar with reasonable dexterity again—to come on board with his new outfit, which he named the Rest.

Ozzy, too, had decided (in the absence of any other options) to become a singer, and while some time would pass before he met his future bandmates, their paths were—given the small but industrious Birmingham music scene—likely to cross before too long. The budding singer went through a few more or less unremarkable bands—the Prospectors, the Black Panthers, Music Machine, and Approach among them. By 1968, all of these had failed, leading him to place an ad on the musicians' noticeboard at the local Ringway Music Store:

"Ozzy Zig requires gig. Owns own PA."

This was not a barefaced lie: he had bought the aforementioned public address system, which consisted of a set of Vox speakers, a microphone, and a stand, from George Clay's music shop on Broad Street.

OPPOSITE: *Hard-rock band Mythology, inspired by Cream and Jimi Hendrix, photographed in 1968.*

The ad was read with interest by one Geezer Butler, who was now playing rhythm guitar in a band called the Rare Breed, in which he was joined by lead guitarist Roger Hope, Mick Hill on bass, and Tony Markham on drums. Rare Breed played covers of psychedelic tunes and was fronted for some time by a singer called John Butcher. By the summer of '68, Butcher had grown dissatisfied with the band and quit, prompting Butler to contact Ozzy in hopes of recruiting him.

This meant that two key bands—the Rest and the Rare Breed—were now occupying the Birmingham covers-band circuit. Nothing stayed the same for long in this evolving scene, of course, and it wasn't long before the former split up. While Ozzy and Butler pondered their next move, Rare Breed

BELOW: *Tony Iommi performing with Jethro Tull in the recording of the* Rolling Stones Rock and Roll Circus *movie in 1968.*

changed its name to Mythology and began to explore hard-rock territory, inspired by Cream and Jimi Hendrix, then two of the loudest musical entities in existence.

Concerts during the summer of 1968 in northern towns such as Halifax, Chester, and Manchester allowed Mythology to build a small following. However, the good vibes were spoiled by a police raid on the band's rehearsal room, leading to the entire band being arrested for possession of cannabis. Iommi and Ward were given two-year conditional discharges and £15 fines. This proved to be the end of Mythology. The band split up in July.

Iommi and Ward both knew Butler, who had by now switched to bass guitar, and invited him to form a band with them. The latter recommended his recent bandmate in Rare Breed, Ozzy Osbourne, as a singer, along with saxophonist Alan Clarke and a second guitarist, Jim Phillip. The Polka Tulk Blues Band, as the new sextet called itself, began rehearsals; the name is said to have come from Ozzy, who either saw it on a tin of talcum powder or took it from the name of a Pakistani clothes shop in Aston (he seems to have forgotten which story is accurate).

Ward and Butler became close friends, with the drummer constantly amused by Butler's buffoonish behavior. As he told me, "There was a period when we first started hanging around together. We were in the dressing room together, and I was lying back on a couch—you know, I was pretty high at the time—and Geezer came in, and he was trying to climb up this fuckin' wall! He kept falling down, but he kept running up the wall and falling on his ass. And I'm just watching this repeatedly and thinking, 'I've gotta get to know this guy.' He was laughing, you know, because he kept falling down. I've had so many good times with that man."

By his own admission, Butler was also not exactly the world's greatest bass player— not yet, anyway. "Back then I was terrible," he recalled. "I'd never even thought about bass! I was literally looking over at Tony and playing the root note of whatever chord he was playing at the time. The first time I ever played bass was at a gig. I couldn't afford a real bass, so I just tuned the strings down on a Telecaster, and they were flapping all over the place. I just played A, B, E—no runs whatsoever—and I had a lot of catching up to do, especially because in those days we only had one gig a week if we were lucky."

In the interim, he spent his time honing his playing style, inspired by bands like the Who ("Every bass player quotes the bass solo in 'My Generation'"), the Beatles ("McCartney's bass playing is unique—I learned some of his bass-lines and they're so emotional, especially on the song 'Something.'"), and Cream.

"I just spent my whole time practicing bass and listening to Jack Bruce," he recalled. "I used to love the bass line on Cream's 'Spoonful,' but I couldn't even get my fingers around the strings of that Fender VI he used to play, because it was so small. I'd never seen anyone use bass as a sort of semi-lead instrument, while at the same time being perfectly linked to the drums and the guitar. The way he bent the notes and came down the fretboard was amazing, too."

Over time, Butler would also draw inspiration from the work of jazz players like Charles Mingus, Stanley Clarke, and, in particular, Jaco Pastorius. "He was so innovative: he was such a technical player, and I suppose he was the first guy to play like that. I wasn't into that kind of music, initially—I never even knew it existed. I'd always been told that the bass should be in the background, and played along with the drums, and then Jaco came along and threw away the rules. It was amazing listening to it. You knew you could never come up to his level. You knew what he was doing, and at the same time you know you could never do it yourself!"

DOWN TO EARTH

It soon became obvious that Clarke and Phillip were not meshing well with the rest of the band. Iommi's playing left little room for a second guitar, and the saxophone sounded irrelevant to the heavy blues direction in which the band was moving. After two shows in August 1968—one at the Banklands Youth Club in Workington and the other at Carlisle's County Ballroom—Phillip and Clarke were fired. Now, for the first time, a quartet comprising Ozzy Osbourne, Tony Iommi, Geezer Butler, and Bill Ward was in existence.

Renaming itself Earth, the band adopted an essentially blues-driven sound that got heavier as time passed. A professional infrastructure was sorely needed, though: on one occasion, the foursome arrived to play a Birmingham club booking to be told that the crowd was eager to hear the band's latest single. It soon became apparent that Earth had been mistaken for a much bigger and more successful band of the same name. The crowd's reaction was less than ecstatic as a result.

It's at this point that Jim Simpson, the manager of two bands called Bakerloo Blues Line and Tea and Symphony, enters the story. A trumpet player with a pop band called Locomotive, he had been part of a hit the same year with the song "Rudi's in Love" and was now running a club, Henry's Blues House, on the corner of Hill Street and Station Street. Led Zeppelin had recently made a memorable appearance there, which had not gone unnoticed by the members of Earth, who asked Simpson if they could play there too.

Simpson, who today is still running the Big Bear management company he started in 1968, gave me an extensive interview about this far-off era. "After Henry's Blues House had been running for two or three weeks," he began, "they came up to me and said, 'We've got a band: can we do an audition?' And eventually they did. They struck me as innocent, confused, and a bit directionless; they didn't really know what the next step was. They seemed to have a bit of a following in Cumberland, for some reason. But nobody quite knew how or where."

Simpson arranged for Earth to play a support slot prior to a set by Ten Years

ABOVE: *Poster advertising the* **Rolling Stones Rock and Roll Circus,** *in which Tony Iommi performed with Jethro Tull.*

After in November 1968. "I remember being impressed with the band—so much so that we tried to help them get gigs in London," said Leo Lyons, the headline act's bass player. "I don't know how much help we were, but I heard that Geezer Butler mentioned it in a later interview. He was also quoted as saying that he learned a lot of his bass licks from me. That was kind of him."

Simpson was recruited as Earth's manager in due course. "I got them a few gigs at Henry's," he explained, "and a relationship developed and I started managing them. There wasn't any great emotion about it: the scales didn't fall from my eyes or anything. We sort of slowly oozed into it, because I'd been offering them support and advice leading up to then anyway. It was a natural progression [to be their manager] from having talked to them. The first thing we did was sit down for several days and worry about names, directions, and what we were going to do."

Of course, being a manager meant entering into a professional agreement, so the experienced Simpson drew up a contract

ABOVE: *Boris Karloff starring in the 1963 horror film,*
Black Sabbath.

for the band to sign. This involved talking to
the musicians' parents, and persuading the
Osbourne, Iommi, Butler, and Ward families
that their sons could make a living from music
was no easy task.

"I had to push them to get their parents
to take it all seriously," he recalled. "I went
to meet their parents and I think they all
thought that my enthusiasm was misplaced.
I knew the band was going to make it. There
was no doubt in my mind whatever. But their

mums and dads were a bit bemused by it all,
I think. 'What, our little Tony? How can he be
a star?'

"Apart from Tony," he continued, "they all
thought my enthusiasm was pretty misplaced
anyway, and that they were destined to be
what they always had been—in other words,
broke! But Tony had a bit of a fixation on
becoming a star. He was the one who spoke
most readily. Bill didn't get involved much.
Ozzy seemed to want to speak a lot, but he
was a bit shy in those days."

In September 1968, shortly after Simpson's
appointment as manager, Earth played shows

in Lichfield and Carlisle, as well as a return date at Henry's Blues House. In November, they performed at Mother's Club in Erdington, then in Carlisle once more, and in December in Langholm. However, a serious upset came in December when Iommi quit the band to join Jethro Tull, then as now a well-known, internationally famous folk-rock band. He didn't stay long, fortunately—just long enough to take part in the recording of the Rolling Stones' *Rock and Roll Circus* movie, which took place at Intertel Studios on December 11 and 12. (Visit YouTube today for the sight and sound of the young guitarist surrounded by the biggest stars of the day.)

Returning to Earth—literally—Iommi warned his bandmates that a new level of discipline would be required if they were to compete with the professionalism of the musicians he'd met during his brief Tull sojourn. Rehearsals would now take place early in the day and would need to be attended on time, with songwriting and performing high on the agenda. Simpson organized support slots with Jon Hiseman's Colosseum, John Mayall's Bluesbreakers, and several of Simpson's own bands: Locomotive, the Bakerloo Blues Band, and Tea and Symphony.

He didn't stop there; by early 1969, Simpson had gained Earth a series of overseas bookings, as both headliners and support acts. A trip to Denmark to play at the Brøndby Pop Klub was followed by gigs at the Marquee in London, the Bay Hotel in Sunderland (where Van der Graaf Generator and the DJ John Peel also played), and, in

April, the famous Star-Club in Hamburg. Earth also returned to Hamburg in August for an extended residency.

By now, however, they had settled on a new band name, which was announced at a show at Banklands Youth Club, Workington, on Tuesday, August 26, 1969. They got it from a horror movie released six years earlier, starring Boris Karloff . . .

BELOW: *Poster advertising the 1963 film,* Black Sabbath, *which six years later would inspire the name of a new band.*

HEAVY METAL'S YEAR ZERO

1970

Try to understand what the name "Black Sabbath" meant in the late sixties and early seventies. A lot of impressionable people genuinely believed back then that you could watch a horror film and die of fright, or that you could inadvertently summon a demon by saying the Lord's Prayer backward. Nowadays, of course, we're all so jaded that a whole genre of horror films can call themselves "torture porn" and it's all fine and dandy, but back then it was a wholly different story.

At this point, Jim Simpson had the band moving forward nicely, as any decent manager should. He knew that its live act had to be different to grab the public's attention. "See, the world was full of boring blues bands at the time—with people playing 150-hour-long guitar solos and boring the pants off people," he told me. "Onstage,

OPPOSITE: *A portrait of Black Sabbath outside of a church in 1970.*

people were wearing boots and raggedy jeans. So we decided we weren't going to have any of that: we had to get Sabbath out of that blues mode into something that was more commercial. So we thrashed around off and on, and meanwhile I booked them gigs with people who trusted me enough to take on a band without knowing much about them."

YOUTH AND ENTERPRISE

The next significant development came when Simpson introduced Black Sabbath to an independent producer called Tony Hall, who had his own agency, Tony Hall Enterprises. Impressed by what he heard, Hall suggested that the group record a debut album. A session was booked for late 1969 at Regent Sounds Studio on Tottenham Court Road in London. Hall also put up £500, which would be sufficient for a few hours of recording—or,

as Sabbath saw it, a chance to run through its live set a few times. When that debut album would actually appear remained to be seen, but in January 1970 the Fontana label released a one-off Black Sabbath single, "Evil Woman." By modern standards, the recording of the album, produced by Tony Hall Enterprises' producer Rodger Bain, was so rapid as to seem ludicrous. As Butler told me, "We did the first album in two days. That's the way it should be. The second album was done in five days and the third one in a week, and those were our biggest-selling albums—and are to this day. We literally went into the studio, set up our equipment, and recorded it as a live gig. Tony did a couple of overdubs, solos and things,

OPPOSITE: *A 1970 color portrait of Black Sabbath in London.* **ABOVE:** *The first Black Sabbath single, "Evil Woman," was released by Fontana in January 1970.* **BELOW:** *Black Sabbath's first recording session took place in late 1969 at Regent Sounds Studios on London's Tottenham Court Road.*

afterward, and that was it. We weren't allowed to be in on the mix or anything like that."

Ward added, "What I like about the first album is the swing time, and the very subtle jazz qualities: I also like the sound of the cymbals. It showed off the band's live technique. The recording setup was quite simple—we recorded it in two days!—but we were a band with a full understanding of the frequency spectrum. We were already mastering the highs and the lows live, and we were listening to each other: that really shows up on the first LP. In parts, it's really smooth and tight. We always used a swing feel, right up to the last tour; there were all sorts of tricks that I was getting up to. We were so hot. Everyone listened to jazz drummers back then—we were all doing it. Gene Krupa was the main one: he was a real dyed-in-the-wool influence for me."

"We were probably nervous," Butler added, "but we were excited at the same time. We had a chance to make an album. It was what we'd worked for. We finally had the chance to do it, [although] we played some of the tracks either too slow or too fast because of the excitement, the energy. It was a bit faster than what we normally played.

"We were just used to playing a lot, seven days a week—or seven spots a day. When we used to play in Hamburg, we played a lot—seven three-quarter-of-an-hour spots. You get pretty used to doing stuff like that. When we walked into the studio, it was a luxury to just be able to play and tape it."

The new songs featured lyrics by Geezer Butler, who had become the wordsmith of the band. Iommi was effectively the musical director, and Ozzy and Ward simply fulfilled their roles to the best of their ability—at least according to Simpson, who remembered, "Geezer did a good job. Bill kept great time and drove well, but he had all the trouble he needed to do the job that he did. I like drummers who do the job well, [who don't] overdo it and play too many fills. As for Tony, I knew about his finger injury, of course, but it didn't play a large part by then. He was a very meticulous guitar player; he really planned things carefully. There were times when he'd come offstage and he'd played a different solo than usual. I'd say, 'Good solo, Tony, I see you changed a part'—and he'd say, 'No I didn't, I made a mistake!' And I'd say, 'But you played it in time, you played it within the chord, it was still useful?' But he'd say, 'Yes, but it wasn't what I intended to play. . . .'

"Ozzy was the one who had doubts about his ability," Simpson continued. "He would get very distraught about it. His confidence was very low; he needed reassurance. It's always harder for the singer, because you open your mouth, you make a noise, and you ask yourself if it's any good or not—whereas if you play the trumpet, you play the notes and the scales and the arpeggios and you know you've hit the note. It's more quantifiable. But just because you like someone's voice doesn't mean the next guy's going to like it.

"I can't imagine anyone intimidating Ozzy, because his character and his spirit were indomitable. But I think he could feel crushed by words. Ozzy is the sweetest guy on earth, and if you said something hurtful to him, he'd be hurt. He didn't talk about his family background—we were all besotted with the music."

Indeed they were: writing, rehearsing, performing, and recording these songs, laden heavy with guitar riffs and Satanic majesty as they were, took up everyone's attention. Bill Ward recalled this halcyon period affectionately, saying, "We were playing a lot of gigs, and when we weren't doing that we were sleeping and trying to eat . . . but we were playing in the Marquee Club in Wardour Street every single week, so we were really well-known in London, and we were building noticeability. They were great times—really hard work, though."

After the Regent Street recording session, Jim Simpson began shopping around record companies, looking for a deal, although most of the various executives failed to see anything special in Sabbath's music. As Simpson recalled, he went to see them not once but twice—first with demo tapes, before the LP was recorded, and then with the finished recordings. "I took them personally and got a straight no [from all the labels]. And after Tony [Hall] fronted the money to go and record at Regent Sound, we took what was the finished master for the first album, and I took that 'round as well, and got another fourteen no's!"

Were any of the labels remotely interested? "Oh, some of them listened to as much as three or four minutes of it!" he continued, grimly. "I played as much as I could persuade them to listen to. I was madly enthusiastic about it and,

generally speaking, they were madly bored. Their eyes were glazed and they were looking in the mirror at their permed hair and their gold medallions and adjusting their purple shirts to make sure their chest hair was on display. But this was par for the course in those days. There were a million times more people in the music industry than there is now, but they weren't too thick on the ground."

Against the prevailing evidence, Simpson's efforts paid off. A deal was eventually struck with Vertigo, well known for its fondness for progressive rock and the then-new hard-rock sound. An American deal swiftly followed with Warner Bros.

"Ozzy was the one who had doubts about his ability..."
—JIM SIMPSON

The songs, the artwork, the image, Ozzy's sinister, untrained monotone, Iommi's monolithic riffs . . . it all combined to create the impression of a musical phenomenon far greater than the four scruffy musicians who inhabited it. The public lapped it up, too. *Black Sabbath* made an immediate impact on its release on February 13, 1970, surpassing even the predictions of supporters such as Jim Simpson by climbing to No. 8 in the UK charts and No. 23 in the US. Even the band members themselves hadn't expected it to do so well: Ozzy once said that he would have been content just to show his mother that his voice had ended up on vinyl.

THE UNHOLY TRINITY

Black Sabbath made its presence known before the buyer even placed the LP on the turntable. Vertigo, well known for its experimental sleeve designs, had used an unsettling image of an unidentified, witchlike woman standing in a grim countryside setting, all browns and grays. A poem appears on the inner gatefold, beginning, "Still falls the rain, the veils of darkness shroud the blackened trees, which, contorted by some unseen violence, shed their tired leaves, and bend their boughs toward a gray earth of severed bird wings . . ."

The first song on the album is sometimes referred to as "the unholy trinity of metal"— "Black Sabbath" from *Black Sabbath* by Black Sabbath. Starting with the sound of a rainstorm and a tolling bell (motifs emulated by dozens of heavy metal bands ever since, for example Metallica, with "For Whom the

Bell Tolls," and Slayer, with "Raining Blood"), the song surges suddenly into life with a dronelike riff based on a tritone or *diabolus in musica*. This sinister interval, equating to half an octave, is said to have so spooked religious musicians in the Middle Ages that it was outlawed as "the devil's interval," although of course this tale could be completely untrue. (Still, it's a nice story to tell.) Ozzy's spine-chilling wail of "What is this, that stands before me?" remains the key phrase of this album. Live, it is a moment to cherish.

"Black Sabbath" makes use of a slightly tricky time signature, but Ozzy conquers it. As Bill Ward told me, this ability to spot the pocket and stay in it is something that most observers still fail to associate with Ozzy. "When we do the song 'Black Sabbath,' Ozzy knows where the holes are, but whenever we do that song with another singer, they sing it in time. And when they sing it in time, it becomes out of time, because there *is* no time! They're singing it *properly*. Ronnie James Dio [the post-Ozzy Sabbath singer], for example, sang it properly and in time, but when you sing it in time you'll throw the track out, because it has no rhyme or reason. That song is a great example of that, so with the other singers, things didn't connect."

Other high points on this slightly primitive but enormously influential album include "Behind the Wall of Sleep," an expert exercise in allowing a riff to breathe. It's interesting

LEFT: *The artwork for Black Sabbath's first full album, 1970's* **Black Sabbath**.

to note that there's tangible subtlety in the songwriting, with the riffage replaced at times by a warm, almost pastoral range of tones. As the drums fade out, a wonderful bass solo ("Bassically") from Geezer stretches out for forty seconds, aided by a wah-wah pedal and demonstrating how, in due course, he would become one of British rock's most accomplished bassists.

"N.I.B." is one of the most fully formed songs in the early Sabbath catalogue, switching from the blues of the main riff to a descending chord sequence that is totally Sabbath in tone. Geezer Butler explained the song's unusual title: "Originally it was titled 'Nib,' [after] Bill's beard, which looked like a pen nib because it was pointy, so we used to call him Nib. When I wrote it, I couldn't think of a title for the song, so I just called it 'Nib,' after Bill's beard. To make it more intriguing, I put punctuation marks in there, but by the time it got to America, they translated it to 'Nativity in Black.'"

Black Sabbath is a great album. It's not flawless by any means—the recording budget and the musicians' experience were both too meager for that—but the LP stands tall among any of the great releases that appeared at the beginning of the seventies. Not everybody saw it that way, of course. When Ozzy took the record home to play for his parents, his father made a comment along the lines of, "Are you sure you were just drinking alcohol? This isn't music, this is weird."

Praise indeed. With an album finally under their belts, it was time for the men of Sabbath to take the music to people, and take it they did, packing in the road miles and touring for the rest of 1970. One notable appearance came in March at the Atomic Sunrise Festival at the Roundhouse in Chalk Farm, alongside Alexis Korner, David Bowie with his band the Hype, Genesis, Brian Auger, Hawkwind, Kevin Ayers and the Whole World, and Arthur Brown. How's that for a classic lineup?

Sabbath was now playing larger clubs such as the Marquee in London, as well as university venues that could hold a decent-sized crowd. This sometimes made for a frantic traveling schedule, such as at the end of March, when the band played gigs in London, Hamburg in Germany, and Workington in the northwest of England in the space of three days. Supported by bands such as Hardin and York, Van der Graaf Generator, Caravan, and Taste (featuring the young blues guitarist Rory Gallagher), Black Sabbath slowly carved out a reputation as a powerful live act. European dates followed, but a proposed US tour was delayed after civil rights disputes at various universities had made some promoters nervous about booking rock acts (even if the correlation now seems tenuous at best).

CHANGE OF MANAGEMENT

Trouble was brewing, unfortunately. Annoyed at having to fulfill a series of gig bookings in smaller venues, arranged before the band's profile suddenly went stratospheric, Sabbath grew apart from its manager. Simpson's view—quite reasonable in retrospect—was

THE INSTITUTE, BLACKWOOD
BEAT DANCE
Friday, 22nd May, 1970
Dancing 8 p.m. to 12 midnight

BLACK SABBATH

VERTIGO ALBUM VO6   BIG BEAR MANAGEMENT
021 454 7020

supported by
"ESTHER'S TOMCATS"
now called " LAZY DOLL "

Admission 10/6d.   Free Late Buses

Tickets available from :—
The Dorothy Cafe, Blackwood
Plaza Cafe, Pontllanffraith
Music Centre, 9 Skinner Street, Newport
Sound Centre, 26 High Street Arcade, Cardiff
Sound Centre, 91 Queen Street, Tredegar
Clewer Bros., 4 Marke Street, Caerphilly
and at the door on night of Dance
★ Preference given to ticket holders on this special night ★

ABOVE: *An advertisement for a show headlined by Black Sabbath on May 22, 1970.* OPPOSITE: *Black Sabbath onstage at the Plumpton Festival in Sussex, England, on May 23, 1970.*

bands, and loyalties prevail. If you book the band in and the guy can't pay more than £800, and you decide to accept his £800, if the record goes big you've got to honor these things. You do your best to renegotiate, but the guy deserves some sort of comeback because he booked the band when we needed him to book the band.

"The big fight was really because they thought we should scrap all those bookings and start again," Simpson continued. "Apart from canceling all those, you upset lots of fans who are buying your records. It takes you off the map, because if you arrange a date now it ain't going to happen for another ten or twelve weeks anyway. I was already getting them £800 or £1,000 or £1,200 for [gigs], but once *Black Sabbath* came out, people were prepared to pay £2,000 or £2,500, and those were going in the book. They weren't going in the book for this week or next week, they were booked for seven to ten weeks' time. And that was the big problem we had: it was me trying to convince [the band] that they had to show a certain degree of responsibility. I remember saying to them, 'We need these people on the way up, and we hope they'll be nice to us on the way down!' But, of course, there *was* no way down. . . ."

Approaches were made to the members of Sabbath by the successful and much-feared manager Don Arden via one of his other signings, the Move's Carl Wayne. Although the band members declined Arden's advances on this occasion, they were keen on two of his former staff, Patrick Meehan and Wilf Pine,

that it would be wrong to cancel a booking because the band had since become too big for it, although he did attempt to negotiate more money from the promoters as a gesture toward his band's larger status.

As he recalled, "I'd booked Sabbath into many venues I'd known in the past with other

ABOVE: *Don Arden photographed in March 1968 in London.*

The end came quickly, said Simpson. "It was resolved by them walking out on me. I got a letter. On the Friday night I heard a knock on the front door and Luke, the road manager, said that the band couldn't go to Liverpool that night because they'd got no money. What had been happening—with my approval, by the way—was that they'd been taking all of the fee; you just picked up cash at most gigs and divided it in four. There was no commission being paid. I didn't care, because all the bookings went in the book, and the next time we'd got a check booking, I'd have taken that. We'd just turned the corner, and all the money was just going to start coming in, so I didn't really care whether I got my commission then or in a month's time."

Surprised by the band's lack of cash on the day of the Liverpool gig, Simpson called the musicians. "I said, 'How come you've got no money? You've been taking all the bookings.' They said, 'Well, we've spent it all; if you can't give us 200 quid we can't go to the booking tonight.' So I raised £200 and gave it to them— and that was a lot more money then than it is now, of course!—and off they went to play in Liverpool."

The end came on September 4, 1970, a few days before the release of the second Black Sabbath album, *Paranoid*. "Early the next morning I got a letter from the lawyers saying [words to the effect of], 'We don't want you to contact the band any more, we're handling the band. They want to leave you because you've not been doing your job right.'

who had broken away to set up their own organization. As Simpson remembered, "Wilf Pine and Pat Meehan were Don's enforcers, or whatever the word is. But then Patrick and Wilf walked out on Don. They saw what Don did—how he recruited an artist—and thought, 'Let's do this on our own.' And the first one they went for was Black Sabbath, who Don had [so far] failed to get."

The week they left me, they were No. 1 on the *Music Business Weekly* chart, one of the music industry newspapers at the time along with *Record Retail*. I had a No. 1 album, a No. 16 album—because *Black Sabbath* had come back on the chart again—and a No. 2 single. And I hadn't been doing my job right?"

Simpson subsequently sued the band, commencing a long and arduous process that dragged along for many years. Looking back, he felt the only real winners by the time the case came to court were his legal advisors, who he said had earlier advised him against taking an out-of-court settlement. He felt no resentment toward the band, however.

"I liked Ozzy and I still do; I think he's one of humanity's nicer people," he explained. "He doesn't conform in any way. He's very honest, very loyal, very straightforward, and he was the one who didn't want to leave me when the push came. I've got a lot of time for Ozzy—I think he's a very good man. I've seen him a couple of times and he's been absolutely great. I saw him two or three years ago and he hugged me.

"I've encountered Tony a couple of times, and it's been very formal but friendly. We've both been very dignified, polite, and pleasant to each other—there's no need to be anything else after all these years. I bumped into Geezer at [department store] House of Fraser in Birmingham and he scuttled away. And I

haven't seen Bill. I feel no rancor toward any of them, but I feel real affection to Ozzy still. The guys were doing very well when I was with them, and they would at least have had a reliable, honest, vaguely intelligent manager. To give you an idea, I manage a band called King Pleasure and the Biscuit Boys now. We had a contract in our first eight years together, but after that we didn't bother—and I'm now [over two decades into] managing them. That says something, doesn't it?"

WAR PIGS

Recording of the second Sabbath album, *Paranoid*, was scheduled to begin on June 16, 1970, at Regent Sounds Studio, with Rodger Bain, who had been brought in as producer again by Tony Hall Enterprises, at the controls. Although the LP was recorded in only a matter of days, it spanned three studios, with further sessions taking place at the rather

RIGHT: *1970's* **Paranoid** *was recorded in a matter of days in three different studios. It was released a mere eight months after* **Black Sabbath**.

ABOVE: *Ozzy (left) and Bill at Regent Sound Studio during the* Paranoid *recording session.* **OPPOSITE:** *Ozzy on the piano during the* Paranoid *recording session.*

more sophisticated Rockfield Studios in south Wales, and at Island Studios (now Sarm West) in London. Tom Allom and Brian Humphries were the engineers.

It's a mark of Sabbath's early talent that *Paranoid*, released on September 18, appeared a mere eight months after its predecessor and yet was so full of amazing songs. It has

subsequently gone down in history as one of the most influential metal albums of all time. *Paranoid* also gained Sabbath a wide fan base, including the future Sex Pistols singer John Lydon, who told this author in 2005, "*Paranoid* was one of the best records ever made, a stonker from start to finish. Every single bit of it is a powerhouse."

Bill Ward also recalled, "I like *Paranoid* because we were touring the world at that time—and you can hear the real birth of the band. When Geezer started writing songs like 'Iron Man,' it separated us from everything else that was going on. Everyone else was like, 'What's this?'—and it's very important to look at that, because that was the difference between us and some of the other louder bands at the time. It was the lyrical content as well as the music which made us different, and this album was a pinnacle for us, with songs like 'Hand of Doom.' I loved how we all contributed our parts. *Paranoid* was the jumping-off point. How did I come up with the hi-hat in 'War Pigs'? That was the swing thing again—I'd done exactly the same thing on 'Wicked World,' which appeared on the first album. It was all Buddy Rich!"

In that one paragraph, Ward nails the dark, lustrous appeal of the *Paranoid* album, which remained on the UK chart for eighteen weeks and became Black Sabbath's first No. 1 LP (and its last until 2013). The "Paranoid" single itself was released on August 29 and peaked at No. 4. These are remarkable achievements for a band that had been practically unknown a year before. Its high points are many, including the song "War Pigs," on which Sabbath takes a stance against the warmongering regimes of the day, widely presumed to include the US administration responsible for executing the final stages of the Vietnam War.

Lyrically, the song doesn't break down many barriers (famously, Butler's lyric rhymes "Generals gathered in their masses" with "Just like witches at black masses" . . . no

OPPOSITE: *The full band (top) and Geezer and Tony during the* Paranoid *recording session.* **ABOVE:** *Tony photographed during the* Paranoid *recording session.*

points for invention there), but that's just a part of its charm. At the song's close, Ozzy promises infernal retribution for the war leaders ("Begging mercy for their sins / Satan laughing spreads his wings"). It's little wonder the record company wanted this bit of political commentary minimized, and vetoed the band's initial choice of *War Pigs* as the LP's title.

"Paranoid" is a Sabbath classic through and through. "Finished with my woman 'cause she couldn't help me with my mind," sings Ozzy in his nasal tenor, introducing the themes of sociopathy and psychic decay that made the band's image so simultaneously dark and enthralling. With its catchy main riff noticeably similar to Led Zeppelin's "Communication

Breakdown," released in 1969, the song was the perfect choice of opening single.

It would later emerge that mental illness had inspired the song. As Butler told me in 2005, "I suffered with depression on and off over the years, and it's a hard thing to relate to people. I didn't even know I had it until I had proper tests and got pills to sort it out. People used to think I was just being miserable, but it was actual depression. Originally, and unknown to me, that was what 'Paranoid' was about, the way I was feeling at the time."

Clinical depression wasn't something that was discussed regularly in postwar Aston. "People just didn't ever talk about it: they thought you were literally a nutcase. I used to get told to cheer up all the time. Ozzy's suffered from it on and off, Bill's suffered from it; it was only Tony who escaped it. You just think that it's [a consequence] of boozing or whatever, but it's not; it's a clinical thing, something in your brain. The medication really does the trick—I think it was only when Prozac came out that people really opened up to it.

"I'm the sort of person who doesn't ever switch off thinking about stuff," Butler continued. "I have a terrible time trying to sleep, because I'm always thinking about something. Even though there's absolutely nothing bad going on in my life, I just can't stop thinking about things. I think if you don't get the proper sleep, it really messes up your life . . . it's hard to say when you're a kid if you've got depression or if you just get pissed off. I always remember one time that was

really bad, and I couldn't explain what the mood was, but there was nobody to talk to about it at the time. They used to tell you to go and take your dog for a walk or something."

"Planet Caravan" is a surprise: a gorgeous ballad laden with echoing textures, it demonstrates the mellower side that lay within the Sabbath songwriting team. That said, if anybody still wondered whether Sabbath was harder and heavier than its contemporaries, "Iron Man" dispels any such doubts. Its carved-in-stone riff and almost comically threatening intro, featuring Ozzy's electronically treated wail of "I am Iron Man!," make the song an instant classic.

FIRST AMERICAN TOUR

An American tour was scheduled to begin after Sabbath completed club dates at venues such as the Brangwyn Hall in Swansea, the Greyhound Blues Club in Croydon, and the King's Head in Romford, Essex. Dates in France, Switzerland, Holland, Belgium, and Sweden, supported by Manfred Mann Chapter III, ensured that Sabbath's message was taken to the European masses, night after night, with the band powering through the set (now chosen from two albums' worth of material) at full steam. Young, aggressive, and eager to prove themselves, the musicians were close to their peak at this point. Occasionally, the madness generated by the band's success spilled over: at one show on October 23 at the Mayfair Ballroom in Newcastle, the crowd invaded the stage and began stealing equipment.

At this point, Sabbath was still playing dates booked by Jim Simpson before his firing. One of these was a headlining slot at the Festival of Contemporary Music at Newark in Nottinghamshire on October 24. The band members were reportedly reluctant to play the show and pulled out, angering the promoter, who had offered them the sum of £325 (compared with the £2,000 or so which they were now accustomed to receiving per show). After legal tussles, a local band called Cherokee Smith replaced Sabbath, and the matter was laid to rest. Two final dates—one at Bournemouth Pavilion and another supporting Emerson, Lake and Palmer at London's Royal Festival Hall—were executed before the band headed to the States.

Sabbath began its US tour at Glassboro State College in New Jersey and moved on to the University of Miami in Florida, Ungano's Ritz Theater on New York's Staten Island, and clubs in New York state, Maine (where the band was supported by power-pop act Badfinger and vaudevillians Mungo Jerry), Ohio (with Iommi's former colleagues Jethro Tull), and California (with Alice Cooper, among others). Once the band arrived on the West Coast, it was as if Sabbath had found its spiritual home: a series of dates at the Whisky a Go Go in Hollywood and the famed Fillmore West in San Francisco enabled them to find the faithful.

After finishing off 1970 with shows in Denmark and Germany, Sabbath began rehearsals for its third new album in under two years. Improbably, given the band's relatively fledgling status, it would be a third classic in a row.

OPPOSITE: *Ozzy performing live onstage in Denmark in December 1970.* **BELOW:** *A color photograph of Black Sabbath in 1970.*

RIGHT: *The members of Black Sabbath photographed in 1973; from left to right, they are drummer Bill Ward, guitarist Tony Iommi, singer Ozzy Osbourne, and bassist Geezer Butler.*

3

SNOWBLIND

1971–1978

Master of Reality, recorded at Island Studios in February to April 1971, is a milestone by anyone's standards.

"This is the most enduring Black Sabbath album for me," said Bill Ward. "The production is extremely good. Tony was trying a lot of new things, and I'm very pleased with the drumming. I was pulling off a lot of new things that I'd been trying to do for three years, such as my double-bass work in 'Children of the Grave.' There's a lot of different bass drum movement, and I play the timbale with my left hand on that song too. I was also experimenting more with percussion overdubs. 'Into the Void' was almost the first song that sounded like grunge, or the modern metal of today, with the way I was cutting Tony's guitar in with my hi-hats, and my single-stroke rolls. The songs sound amazing live; they're an absolute blast to play. I have a great time playing drums with Black Sabbath—and always have done."

OPPOSITE: The members of Black Sabbath photographed around October 1973.
ABOVE: Master of Reality, released in 1971, was Black Sabbath's third studio album in a year.

THIS SPREAD: *Black Sabbath on tour in Amsterdam in December 1971 (clockwise from opposite top): Ozzy, Bill, Tony, and Geezer.*

As Geezer Butler told me, "With *Master of Reality*, we wanted to change the music a bit, because we didn't want to keep playing the same stuff all the time. We all bought different instruments, Tony started playing piano; we wanted to expand our musical horizons a bit. So we took our time [because] we could afford to by then. I think the music was better with more money and more time. We'd done so much touring in such a short time by then, that we were all absolutely knackered anyway, and we needed it—we couldn't just come off the road after six months and go straight into rehearsal. So we took the time out to write new stuff. The first two albums came out of a lot of the jamming we did around the clubs: we had the basics of *Paranoid* done by the time we did the first album. That's why they were only six months apart."

After a month's break, during which Ozzy married his girlfriend Thelma Mayfair and became stepfather to her son Elliot, Sabbath plunged into its 1971 touring schedule. The dates had been scheduled to begin on January 5 with a booking at London's Royal Festival Hall alongside Freedom and Curved Air, only for friction to develop between the venue management and the band, with the former stating that "unruly fans were standing on the chairs and causing damage to the venue." Perhaps these noble venues weren't quite ready for Black Sabbath . . .

Shows in Australia and the United States came next, but were hindered somewhat when a stopover between the two countries in Japan, scheduled to take place on February 3, was canceled after the band members were denied entry visas. Ozzy's criminal past catching up with him, maybe? No matter: another lucrative jaunt around North America awaited, kicking off in mid-February in New Jersey and progressing through no fewer than fourteen US states and Canadian provinces. Support slots with the phenomenally successful Fleetwood Mac helped Sabbath's American profile to rise still higher, although how the two bands were supposed to woo a single audience is a mystery, given their disparate musical styles.

Master of Reality appeared on July 21, right after Sabbath performed with the Amboy Dukes, the Seigal-Schwall Band, Alex Taylor, and Brownsville Station in Detroit (and just prior to dates on the East Coast and in Toronto with Yes, Black Oak Arkansas, and Alice

Cooper). The album begins with an ode to marijuana, "Sweet Leaf," introduced by the sound of someone (reportedly Iommi) taking a hit on a bong and coughing, the sound taped, looped, and panned slowly across the speakers. The next song, "After Forever," seems to be advocating a Christian belief, with lines such as "Perhaps you'll think before you say that God is dead and gone" coming in stark contrast to Sabbath's devilish image.

Elsewhere, Iommi's mellower side is on full display: see "Orchid," a short instrumental that lasts just a minute and a half and is effectively an acoustic guitar symphony. The immense "Lord of This World" and "Into the Void," however, are based on all-time classic riffs. Evidently success hadn't taken away any of Iommi's desire to make heavy music.

ICICLES WITHIN MY BRAIN

With the astounding triple-volley of punches that was *Black Sabbath*, *Paranoid*, and *Master of Reality*, the men of Black Sabbath had distinguished themselves beyond all reasonable expectations. They weren't done yet, though. As was often the case in those days, the band worked as hard as it could to make an impact, releasing albums every year (or even more often than that, as we've seen), while remaining firmly on the road.

By May 1972, Sabbath was in the studio yet again, this time to make *Volume 4*. In the interim, Ozzy had become a father for the first time, his daughter Jessica Starshine Osbourne arriving in January. This time, the band was recording at Hollywood's Record Plant—something of an indication of where its members now felt they belonged. A US tour followed, and let us be under no illusion: this was the beginning of the era of Sabbath's heaviest period of rock 'n' roll indulgence (or, at least, the first time that the musicians' experiences with cocaine and booze were to be publicized).

Black Sabbath spent three months crisscrossing the United States —stopping off at the Pocono International Raceway in July for a notable show with Humble Pie, Three Dog Night, Emerson, Lake and Palmer, the Faces, the J. Geils Band, Badfinger, and others—

ABOVE: *The artwork for Black Sabbath's fourth studio album,* Volume 4. BELOW: *Black Sabbath backstage at a show in London in 1972.*

building to the release of *Volume 4* (actually written as *Vol 4* on the sleeve) on September 25. One credit in the liner notes—"We wish to thank the great COKE-Cola company of Los Angeles"—made it clear where the band was headed. Indeed, as Iommi recalled in his 2011 autobiography, *Iron Man*, Sabbath were now taking to having cocaine delivered to the studio, hidden inside speaker boxes.

Oddly, while the credits also indicate that

"It was a great atmosphere—good times, great coke!"
—GEEZER BUTLER

the new album was self-produced, manager Patrick Meehan is given a co-production credit. Who knows: perhaps his influence had led the musicians to be more adventurous? This certainly seems to be the case on "Changes," a piano-and-strings ballad. "Supernaut" is an up-tempo rock anthem based on a harmony riff and huge cymbals from Ward, while "Snowblind" is an anthem to cocaine: "Feeling happy in my pain / Icicles within my brain," Ozzy intones.

"Laguna Sunrise" is another sweet instrumental, although some fans disliked its strings-heavy ambience. It works perfectly in context, showcasing once more Iommi's many-

LEFT: *Ozzy Osbourne posing with a spoon around 1973, a year in which the band's rock 'n' roll indulgence became excessive.*
OPPOSITE: Sabbath Bloody Sabbath, *released in 1973, is cited as one of the peaks of Black Sabbath's talent.*

sided writing talents, but it's an example of how *Volume Four* could and did leave a fair few Sabbath followers more than a little confused. It was less easy to categorize as a "Black Sabbath record," but on the other hand, the musicianship is superior to anything the band members had produced before, and they had also successfully expanded their lyrical approach.

As time has passed, *Volume Four* songs such as "Snowblind" and "Changes" have become set-list perennials. And it's a great LP, if a slightly unusual one. It made No. 8 in the UK and went gold in the States within eight weeks of its release. A UK tour planned for November was canceled due to illness, however: Iommi had the flu, Ward cited "total physical and mental exhaustion," and Ozzy was suffering from laryngitis. As the singer explained, "I was very ill when we returned from the States. I had a septic throat and a temperature of 105 degrees. I was out of action for a month."

It could have been worse—and, in fact, things were about to get *much* worse.

BLOODY SABBATH

"I'd reached a point where I was addicted to narcotics," said Bill Ward mournfully, when I asked him what he recalled of the recording of *Sabbath Bloody Sabbath* in 1973. Geezer Butler saw things differently. "It was a great atmosphere—good times, great coke! Just like a new birth for me," he told me, which reveals, if nothing else, that perspective is everything.

The pace certainly wasn't letting up. In

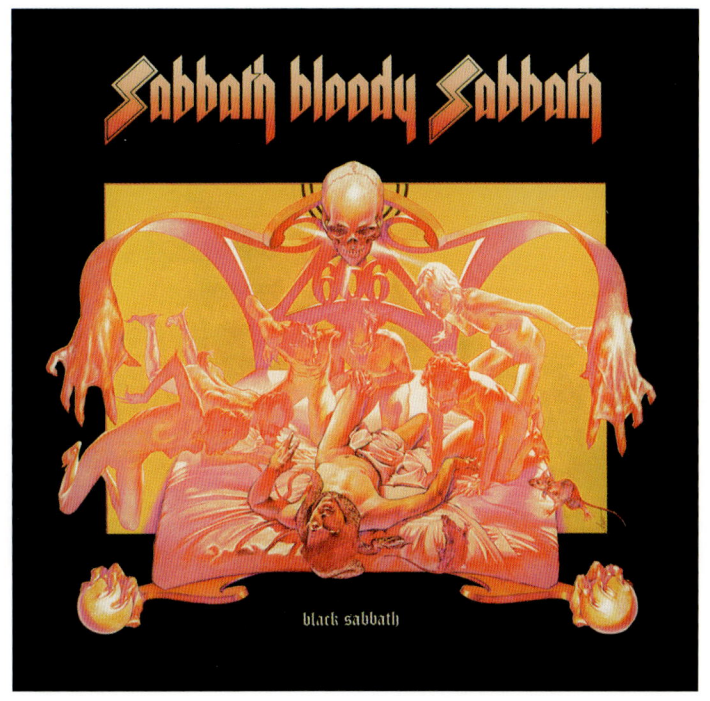

early '73, Sabbath put in yet another row of international dates, this time in New Zealand, with Fairport Convention in tow. Curiously, the second support act was local heroes Split Enz, whose founders would make a huge impact in the 1980s and '90s when the core duo of Neil and Tim Finn formed Crowded House. After gigs in Australia, Sabbath spent February and March on an extended European and UK tour. Check YouTube for evidence of how, substances notwithstanding, the band was on incredible form: little wonder its reputation as a live act of great power was on the rise.

However, this didn't exactly leave much gas in the creative tank when it came to writing new material. After a spell in a house in Bel Air, rented for songwriting purposes, produced zero results due to writer's block and exhaustion on Iommi's part, Sabbath switched locations to Clearwell Castle, an ancient country manor in the Forest of Dean in Gloucestershire. Apparently re-inspired by the grim surroundings, where tales of hauntings

were rife, the band came up with a set of inspired songs that would prove its most compositionally ambitious yet.

Asked many years later what the high point of his songwriting career was, Butler replied, "The song 'Sabbath, Bloody Sabbath' itself.

It was a whole new era for us. We felt really open on that album." Furthermore, Ward reasoned, "By the time we recorded this LP, we'd done multiple tours across the world and we were experienced musicians. We'd matured, although we'd been digesting large amounts of Peruvian marching powder for a while. . . . The drum tracks might have been more technically precise if I hadn't been using drugs, but I look back and I think I did okay: the title track is great to play live. There's a bit at the end with a nice percussion thing going on. By this time we were allowing more things to come into the music—some strings, some brass band. We were moving toward different places; Tony even played a jazz part. We've played with lots of modern bands—Slayer, In Flames, the Haunted, Slipknot, Marilyn Manson—and when we do these songs, they fit right in. They're almost ageless."

Sabbath Bloody Sabbath, with its wonderfully psychedelic artwork and mysterious "Direction: Patrick Meehan" credit on the sleeve, was released on December 1, 1973. Standout tracks include the title song, which kicks off with one of Iommi's best and best-known riffs. Then there's "Sabbra Cadabra," a chunk of melodic rock 'n' roll. The most impressive cut, technically speaking, is "Spiral Architect," which brings the LP to a grandiose ending, with its lustrous string accompaniment (credited to the Phantom Fiddlers) and triple-tracked vocals. Believe it or not, Iommi also contributed bagpipes to the song.

In late '73, Sabbath split with Patrick Meehan, for reasons that seem essentially to boil down to the band-members having signed contracts when they were young, broke, and stupid. "It was horrible," Butler told me. "We had to pay him off. The way he had us tied up in his contracts, we had

OPPOSITE: *Ozzy and Tony onstage during a concert in London in November, 1973.* ABOVE: *Bill at the drum set during a concert in 1973.*

to pay him to get away from him. We didn't have lawyers or anything when we signed the contracts, because we didn't know. . . . We were clueless about business—we just wanted to play music. When we started out, we didn't ever think of making and selling albums anyway. It was just like a hobby to us—anything to avoid the nine-to-five jobs.

We didn't ever once think that it would turn into anything money-making."

By January 1974, new management had been secured in the intimidating form of Don Arden, who was connected to both previous management teams, since he was Meehan and Pine's former employer, and would later become friends with Jim Simpson. Ozzy soon struck up a friendship with Arden's eighteen-year-old daughter, Sharon, who worked as a

OPPOSITE: *A portrait of Ozzy relaxing with his feet up, around 1972.* ABOVE: *Black Sabbath with gold records after the release of* Sabbath Bloody Sabbath. RIGHT: *Black Sabbath in a recording studio, circa 1974.*

RIGHT: *Geezer Butler high-kicking while playing bass during the Chicago concert.* **BELOW:** *A Black Sabbath fan, photographed at the California Jam on April 6, 1974.* **OPPOSITE:** *Black Sabbath backstage at a concert in Chicago on February 11, 1974.*

receptionist in his office—a friendship that deepened over time.

Back in business, Sabbath hit the road in support of *Sabbath Bloody Sabbath*, performing in Sweden, Denmark, Holland, Germany, and Switzerland before embarking on a long US tour in February. A Long Island show saw the band headline over Bedlam, featuring a supremely talented drummer named Cozy Powell, before what was undoubtedly the most ambitious live gig of Sabbath's career to date: the California Jam on April 6, 1974, at the Ontario Raceway in California.

The headliners, Emerson, Lake and Palmer, plus Sabbath and Deep Purple, were asked to play (after the biggest bands of the day, the Rolling Stones, Led Zeppelin, and the Band, had asked for astronomical fees that proved too much) over a bill including Earth, Wind & Fire, Rare Earth, Black Oak Arkansas, Seals and Crofts, and the Eagles. A staggering 200,000 people arrived, each of them paying $10 for a ticket, at a venue that had been chosen for its accessibility to Los Angeles, San Diego, and Orange County, and which boasted parking for 50,000 cars.

Deep Purple bassist Glenn Hughes was an old friend of Sabbath's from the early days, and he could hold his own when it came to partying, to say the least. As he recalled in his autobiography (co-written with the author of this book) in 2011, "I met up with my dear friends Tony Iommi and Ozzy Osbourne of Black Sabbath, and we got some coke and stayed up all night on the 5th, the night before the Cal-Jam. So what you see on the Cal-Jam footage on the 6th is a Glenn Hughes who's been up all night, and it was still a monumental show. It was working for me

then: when you're twenty-two you can stay up all night and hang out, and it's fine."

"Glenn is a great guy," Ozzy recalled. "He's a great singer, man. I remember . . . we all had loads of white powder, and everybody was fucked up on the plane. I was just lying there thinking, 'I'm gonna die when I get off this plane.' And Glenn said, 'You may need a bit of this. . . .'"

Now that would have been a night to remember. Huge events like the Cal-Jam

OPPOSITE: *Ozzy on stage during the California Jam, Black Sabbath's most ambitious and high-profile event at the time.* ABOVE: *The members of Black Sabbath performing at the Cal Jam in April 1974.* RIGHT: *Deep Purple bassist Glenn Hughes at Cal Jam.*

ushered in a new era of rock on a massive scale, although the members of Sabbath would not feel so assured when they discovered how little they actually owned in the wake of the split with Meehan.

GOOD FOR BUSINESS

The band's next album, *Sabotage*, was recorded in early 1975 at Morgan Studios in London and named in angry response to the issues the band had faced. It was the first Sabbath LP to be produced by Iommi, although the overall credit went to Sabbath with Mike Butcher.

The high point of *Sabotage* is the majestic "Symptom of the Universe"—six and a half minutes of riffs, soloing, and key and tempo changes underpinning high-pitched vocals.

ABOVE: Sabotage *was the band's sixth studio release and the first to be produced by Iommi.* BELOW: *A posed group shot of Black Sabbath taken around 1975.*

At 4:30, the song resolves into a piano and acoustic section, and in doing so becomes possibly the first progressive metal song. The vocals were a problem, however. "We always try to get Ozzy to sing 'Symptom of the Universe,'" Butler told me, "but he never will: he says that he can't reach the notes." I suggested that Sabbath could try playing the song in a lower key. "That's what we say, but he still won't. It's a psychological thing, I think. He won't do it."

The road was calling again, and Sabbath finished off 1975 with another European and American tour. Business might have been good, but for some reason or other—the drugs? The pressure? The rise of punk?— Sabbath was not to record a truly excellent album for some years. A compilation, *We Sold Our Soul for Rock 'n' Roll,* was released in late 1975 and went some way toward reminding the kids what a tremendous early catalog

Bill Ward (above) and
Tony Iommi (right)
photographed on
tour in Amsterdam on
January 11, 1975.

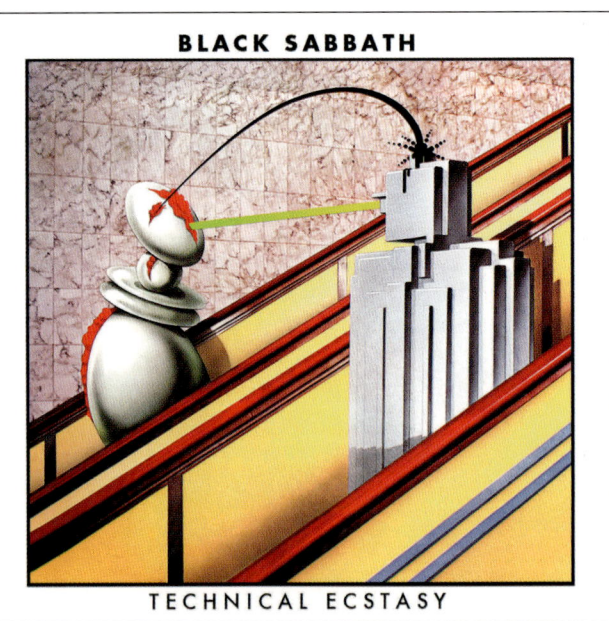

TOP: *Tony Iommi (left) and Ozzy Osbourne on tour in Amsterdam on January 11, 1975.* ABOVE: *A compilation album, We Sold Our Soul for Rock 'n' Roll, was released in 1975. It was followed the same year with the seventh studio album, Technical Ecstasy, which was overshadowed by the rise of punk.* OPPOSITE: *Black Sabbath on tour in Boston in December 1976.*

Sabbath had, but the next studio album, *Technical Ecstasy*, simply didn't match up.

Written at Ridge Farm Studios near Horsham in Surrey, recorded and mixed at Criteria Studios in Miami, and mastered in California, the LP—released on September 25, 1975—was almost devoid of classic riffage, instead focusing on lighter, radio-friendly rock. Although the LP reached No. 13 in Britain, it only remained on the charts for six weeks before dropping off entirely—a far cry from the forty-two and twenty-seven weeks achieved by *Black Sabbath* and *Paranoid*, respectively.

The tour dates were just as relentless as ever, though: for six months straight, starting in October 1976, Black Sabbath hit the road for a huge American and European tour, starting in Tulsa, Oklahoma. Back home in March '77, Sabbath played the UK and

Europe again, this time with AC/DC. The bill was made notable by a backstage incident involving Geezer Butler and AC/DC's rhythm guitarist and principal songwriter, Malcolm Young: the former is reported to have drawn a switchblade comb from his pocket, causing Young to misconstrue it as a pocket-knife, resulting in a drunken argument.

These were the least of Sabbath's problems in late 1977. Ozzy's father, Jack, was seriously ill with cancer, and as the end approached, the singer decided to quit the band. Iommi immediately recruited a singer called Dave Walker, from the band Savoy Brown, but the two singers could not have been more different, either in looks or singing style.

The prospect of an Ozzy-less Black Sabbath seemed not to deter the new lineup, which had begun rehearsing material for its next album along with session keyboard player Don Airey. The Walker-fronted band even appeared on a BBC TV show, *Look Hear*, performing a new song, "Junior's Eyes," written for Ozzy. The show was broadcast

OPPOSITE: *Ozzy performing at the Hammersmith Odeon during the UK and European leg of the tour of 1976–1977.*
BELOW: *Ozzy's replacement in Black Sabbath in 1977 was Dave Walker, a singer who could not have been more different, either in looks or singing style.*

on January 6, 1978, three weeks before Ozzy asked if he could rejoin the band; his father's death had left him in need of emotional release, it seemed. Shortly afterward, he was reinstated, but only temporarily.

The problem now was that Sabbath had lost ground in the face of a tedious last album and the rise of newer, cooler variants of heavy metal. The band's next LP, *Never Say*

LEFT: *Black Sabbath's eighth studio album was* Never Say Die!*, an album that fans and critics liked no more than* Technical Ecstasy. **BELOW:** *Tony Iommi during the Black Sabbath–Van Halen tour of 1978.*

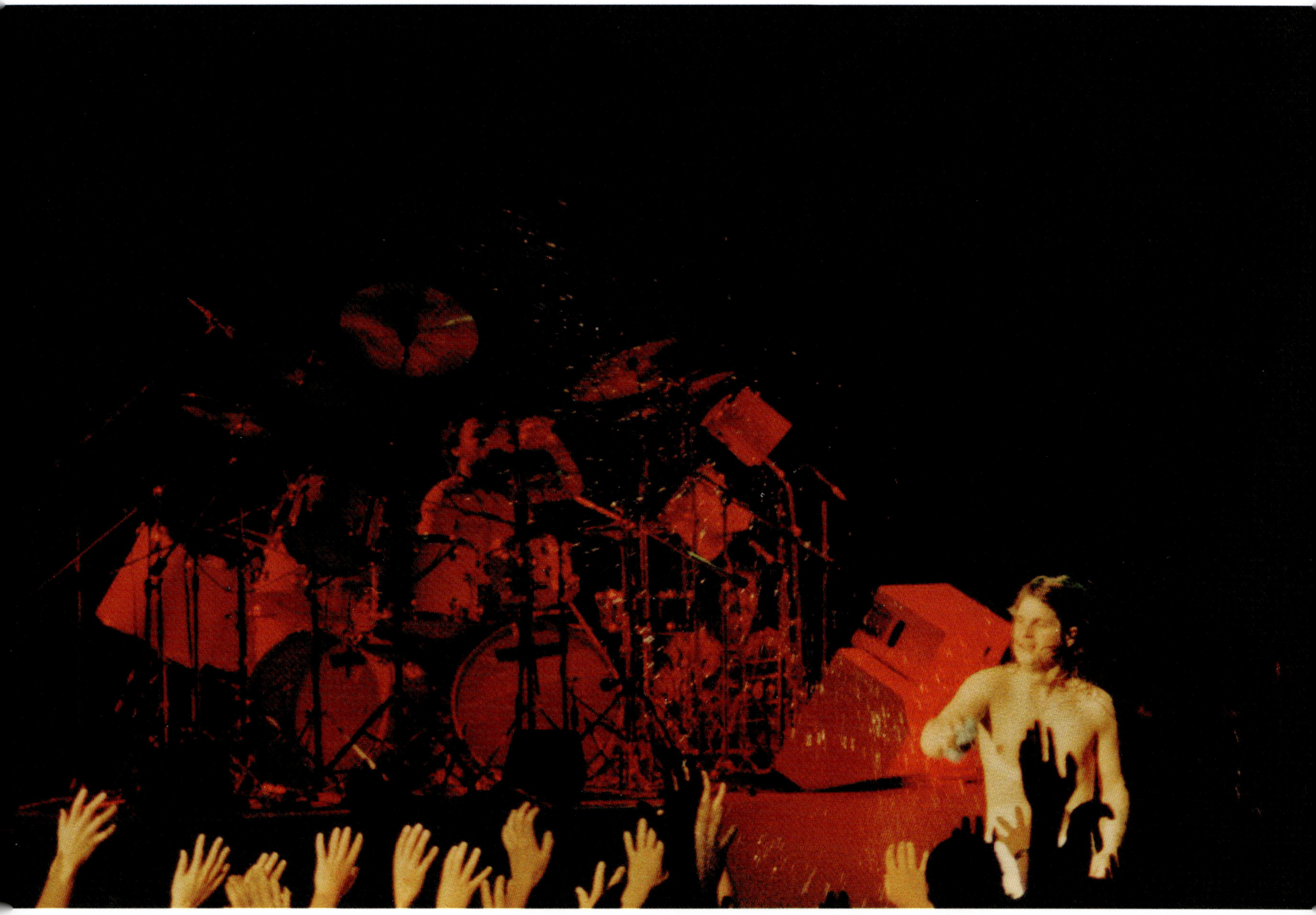

ABOVE: ***Ozzy sprays the crowd of the Hammersmith Odeon with water during the UK leg of the*** **Never Say Die!** ***tour.***

Die!, was recorded in early 1978 at Sound Interchange Studios in Toronto, Canada, and was no better than *Technical Ecstasy* in the eyes of fans and critics.

"*Never Say Die!* was the most difficult Sabbath LP," Ward later recalled. "We were tired, and we were starting to fall apart. It was a horrible time . . . I was in the grip of a progressive illness, and I had to drink every day: I had no choice. Still, the drums came through, regardless of my condition . . . our circumstances as a band and individuals were beginning to change. It's easy to do good things when everything's going great, but it's hard to make something good when everything is falling to pieces—and that shows the victory and the power of this band."

It's perhaps too easy to dismiss *Never*

OPPOSITE: *Tony Iommi, with an effects pedalboard, and Ozzy Osbourne performing onstage in August 1978.* **ABOVE:** *Photo of the members of Van Halen on their tour bus during the Black Sabbath–Van Halen tour of 1978.*

Say Die! as the last effort of a band that had simply run out of enthusiasm. It's certain, however, that Sabbath's decision to choose Van Halen as its support act for the *Never Say Die!* tour was a good one. This young rock quartet from Pasadena, California, was one of the hottest bands on the planet, whereas Sabbath seemed ponderous and tired by comparison.

As writer Sylvie Simmons, who witnessed Van Halen's rise, told me, "Van Halen were almost like a one-off blip. They came out of Pasadena with this thrust of power, which absolutely knocked you sideways. It was absolutely fantastic; they were this completely don't-give-a-fuck band. And of course they toured with Sabbath on that last tour they did, and blew them out of the water. The heavy

ABOVE: *The members of Black Sabbath enjoy cake to celebrate the band's tenth anniversary.* OPPOSITE: *Ozzy performing at the Hammersmith Odeon in London in 1978.*

rock scene at that time was incredibly flaccid— it was all Foreigner and that kind of stuff. Kansas, Boston, REO Speedwagon . . . stadium rock was pretty much dead in the water."

The Sabbath–Van Halen tour played European shows in October before returning to the States in November. On November 16, Ozzy went missing before a show at the Municipal Auditorium in Nashville, Tennessee. As Van Halen singer Dave Lee Roth later recalled in his 1997 book *Crazy*

from the Heat, he and Ozzy had spent the previous night taking coke "until about nine-thirty in the morning" before driving from Memphis to Nashville and checking into a hotel. "It was noontime, and I went right into the bin, fell asleep. Got up, we opened, sold-out show, 10,000 of our closest friends. We're sitting backstage, and suddenly, two of the guys from Black Sabbath and some muscle burst through the door, 'Where is Ozzy? . . . We're not even sure he checked into the hotel.

We can't find him anywhere. We can't do the show.'" It emerged that Ozzy had fallen asleep in the wrong room and then overslept, causing Sabbath to cancel the show.

This might be a fun rock 'n' roll story, but this kind of thing derails bands in the end, especially when they're on the downward slope. Sure, a new album—tentatively titled *Heaven and Hell*—was planned, but Ozzy's heart wasn't in it.

Songwriting sessions, once again in Bel Air, failed to produce anything of note, and on April 27, 1979, Bill Ward was given the job of telling Ozzy that he was fired.

4

HELL'S MADMEN

1979–1981

As one of the world's best-known singers but simultaneously a man lacking in confidence, there was only one real option open to Ozzy Osbourne when he was booted out of Black Sabbath in 1979, which was to hit the bottle—hard. Depressed by the lackluster *Never Say Die!* and already in thrall to addiction, he whiled away a period of weeks or even months slumped in a hotel room, drunk, stoned, or, frequently, both.

It was Sharon Arden who pulled him out of it. Ozzy's future wife had learned a lot from her father Don and suggested that she become the ousted singer's manager. In this way he could set up a solo career with new musicians—and play his former Sabbath bandmates at their own game. He later described Sharon's intervention as "a kick up the ass and a smack in the teeth from my management."

OPPOSITE: *An outtake from the* Blizzard of Oz *photoshoot in 1981. The album launched Ozzy's solo career after his dismissal from Black Sabbath.* **ABOVE:** *Ozzy Osbourne, photographed in Los Angeles in 1979—a dark time when the ousted Black Sabbath singer turned to alcohol.*

ABOVE: *Sharon Arden (left) and Ozzy in a 1978 photograph. The two were close, even before she became his manager (and future wife).*

Guided by his lover and mentor (why yes, it *is* an odd combination), he began to plan his next move.

MOVING ON

At the same time, the remaining members of Black Sabbath—Tony Iommi, Geezer Butler, and Bill Ward, in order of dominance over the band's affairs—were not waiting around. The band's new singer was Ronnie James Dio, a warbler of unearthly vocal prowess who had hit the big time in the mid-to-late seventies with Rainbow, the band formed by Deep Purple's Ritchie Blackmore. Dio's arrival was beset by a certain amount of chaos; Geezer Butler quit Sabbath temporarily after Ozzy's departure, apparently unsure whether anyone could fill the longtime singer's boots.

Butler would later tell me that he felt that

remaining in the band in the period directly after the split was impossible. "When Ozzy left, everybody was really down. I left just after Ozzy, because I felt I couldn't really go on without him, and I had loads of things to sort out in my own life." Had he stayed away, it would have meant that Iommi and Ward were left with the task of finding a bassist *and* a lyricist, so it's just as well that he returned in short order.

It would prove a little difficult for some of Sabbath's fans to accept Dio as front man, given the radical differences between the two singers' voices. Some of the early Sabbath songs gained their sinister nature from Ozzy's untrained, threatening monotone, which often wavered around the correct note in unsettling fashion. Conversely, Dio's voice was a thing of

BLACK SABBATH

HEAVEN AND HELL

BELOW: *Ronnie James Dio was Ozzy's replacement in Black Sabbath, a change that was difficult for fans to accept.*
ABOVE: Heaven and Hell, *Black Sabbath's ninth studio album, was the first that did not have the four original members.*

operatic beauty, delivering spiraling melodies like a kind of rock 'n' roll choirboy.

Recording sessions for the new lineup's debut album, *Heaven and Hell*, began at Criteria Studios in Miami in September 1979, without Butler, who was still on a temporary break from Sabbath. Later recordings took place at Studio Ferber in Paris. An acquaintance of Iommi's named Geoff Nicholls, who played in a band called Quartz, stepped in on bass, switching to the position of touring keyboard player when Butler returned a few days later. The errant bassist soon sensed a real synergy between Dio and the other musicians: as he later told me, "Ronnie brought a lot to the band at a time when we needed it. He gave the band a whole lease of life. He gave everybody inspiration!"

Martin Birch, who had engineered several early Fleetwood Mac and Faces albums,

as well as producing five Deep Purple LPs, was brought in to produce *Heaven and Hell*. He gave the album—released on April 25, 1980—a slick, precise feel that was a step up from previous Sabbath releases, not least in its radio-friendly song arrangements. The obvious example of this new, taut sound was "Neon Knights," a catchy opener with remarkable vocal melodies, and "Children of the Sea," an anthem that opens with an ocean of acoustic guitars. Elsewhere, "Heaven and Hell" is riffier in nature, recalling the glory days of "Iron Man," and so is "Die Young," with its complex midsection.

Heaven and Hell was the perfect antidote to Sabbath's humdrum albums from the last years of Ozzy's tenure. It climbed to No. 9 in the UK at the start of a twenty-two-week residency in the charts. A lengthy tour followed the release, taking in Germany and Austria before UK dates supported by Angel Witch—one of the leading lights of the New Wave of British Heavy Metal (NWOBHM) movement—and Girlschool, the all-female metal group.

However, Bill Ward, whose parents had both died in recent months, was finding life in Sabbath tough to endure. Alcohol had become essential for him by this stage and now, in urgent need of rehab, he left Sabbath on August 21, quitting the band before a show at the McNichols Sports Arena in Denver, Colorado. Support act Blue Öyster Cult played an extended set in Sabbath's absence.

A few years ago, I asked Ward, now decades sober, to define his alcoholism. His

OPPOSITE: *Black Sabbath photographed in Paris during the making of the* Heaven and Hell *album.*
ABOVE: *Black Sabbath with singer Ronnie James Dio at the Gaumont Theatre in Southampton, England, on June 25, 1980.*
RIGHT: *Bill Ward bids farewell to the crowd at the Gaumont Theatre in June 1980. He would leave the band two months later to deal with his addiction.*

ABOVE: *Bill Ward's alcohol and drug addictions led him to leave Black Sabbath in 1980 to focus on getting sober.*

response made it clear why life as a touring musician would eventually have killed him. "My addiction had reached the point where all addictions go to eventually. It had reached the point where it had become more important than anything else in my life. The addiction had become more important than me, more important than my wife at the time, more important than my children, more important than my responsibilities, more important than Black Sabbath, more important than anything. The addiction was king.

"What happened was that I went back to Southern California with my wife, and all I did was drink and use [drugs] and sleep. I stayed in bed for a year directly from *Heaven and Hell*. I very rarely socialized. I pulled the shades down and . . . that was it. I was dealing with grief. I was dealing with all kinds of problems. I didn't know at the time, but today I can look back and go, 'Yes, I was dealing with this and that. . . .' But I didn't do that at the time. I didn't realize that I was in the grip of a progressive illness that was going to kill me. I had no idea of what was ahead because it got definitely worse from that point. That was bad enough, but it got a lot worse than that."

Understanding the nature of his problem was the key to recovery. "There's such a thing as heavy drinkers, you know: people who drink heavily but don't become alcoholics. They just drink heavily. It almost gives the impression that they're alcoholics. An alcoholic, basically, is going to need to drink all the time, and there's two types. What we call a periodic alcoholic—who doesn't drink for a while but then drinks continually, hour after hour. And then there's the daily alcoholic, who drinks every single day. An alcoholic will put alcohol before anything and anybody, whereas a heavy drinker will turn around and say, 'You know what? Fuck this, I'm not gonna drink for another couple of weeks.' He or she makes that decision: an alcoholic can't make that decision."

Ward's replacement was ex-Axis drummer Vinny Appice—a seasoned drummer with highly evolved musical skills. Appice, whose older brother Carmine is also a well-known drummer—having played with Vanilla Fudge and Beck, Bogert & Appice—took the drum stool for the remaining four months of the 1980 tour. "I met Bill at the Rainbow in the eighties, when he was drinking," he told me, "and I ran out the back door, because when I went over to introduce myself he [growled] 'Vinny! Hey!' and put his arms 'round me. He was really drunk, and not really a *good* drunk,

so I was like, okay, time to get out of here . . . exit stage left!"

It may come as a surprise to learn that Appice almost ended up on Team Ozzy, before Sabbath came calling. "It's a funny story," he recalled, "because before they called me, I'd had a call from Sharon Arden a while before, saying that Ozzy was putting a new band together and would I like to fly out? They'd heard me play with Rick Derringer and Axis. I'd done three albums with Rick by then, and the Axis album had really cool drums on there, so they knew I was capable of playing with Ozzy. I was twenty-one years old, and I was like, 'Wow, Ozzy!' But I'd never been to Europe before, and

BELOW: *Black Sabbath, down two original members, continued the* Heaven and Hell *tour apace with Dio as singer and Vinny Appice on the drums.*

I asked my brother Carmine, 'Isn't Ozzy crazy?' Carmine had hung out with Ozzy years before and said, 'Yeah, he's crazy. He's really wild.' So I actually turned it down. I was a kid; I didn't know. I just thought, 'He's a madman, he's crazy, I've never been to England, where's that?'

> ## "I asked my brother Carmine, Isn't Ozzy crazy? Carmine had hung out with Ozzy . . . 'Yeah he's crazy . . .'"
> —VINNY APPICE

"So I turned down that gig and then, about three months later, I was on my way back from a Ludwig drum convention in Chicago with Carmine. My wife Justine told me that the road manager from Black Sabbath had called and wanted me to go and meet with them at their hotel. So I met Paul Clarke, the tour manager at the time, and then Tony Iommi came in. He'd heard the Axis album and really liked it, and wanted to know if I wanted to audition with them the next day at SIR Studios on Sunset Boulevard in Hollywood. So I said yeah, and went down and played and everything went well. They told me Bill was having problems and had left. I don't think they knew I'd been asked to join Ozzy's band before that. . . . They were happy with my audition and they went to the pub, then

LEFT: *Drummer Vinny Appice, photographed in Hammersmith on January 18, 1981, replaced Bill Ward during the* Heaven and Hell *tour.*

came back and said, 'Okay, you're gonna do it: you're in the band!'"

The new drummer was soon put to work. "So now I gotta learn all these songs," he remembered, "and I've only got four days of rehearsals before a big show at the stadium in Hawaii. For the rehearsal on the first day, Geoff Nicholls and Ronnie helped me through the songs, while Tony and Geezer and some of the crew went over to the pub. The same thing happened the next day. Everybody was late. It was like, 'Let's play a little bit and then let's go to the pub.' But I was like, 'Man, I've got to learn these songs!' So I worked with Geoff and Ronnie a lot to learn the songs. We didn't rehearse much in the four days we had.

"Next thing we know, we're in Hawaii. I'm constantly listening to the songs on a Walkman at the time, and we're playing this big festival—a big outdoor show in front of 20,000 people. Luckily I know how to read music, and so I'd made these charts indicating 'verse, chorus, verse' and so on, with notes about 6/8 time and accents and all this stuff, for each song. That got me through half the set, until it started raining and the rain made all the ink run on my book! I couldn't read it, but we got through the show."

BATTLE OF THE BANDS

Sabbath, invigorated by the replacement of its two least effective members, powered through the East Coast states, down through Miami and into the American heartlands, firing on all cylinders. However, serious rivalry came from Ozzy and his new album, *Blizzard of Ozz*, credited (initially) to "Ozzy Osbourne's Blizzard of Ozz" and featuring a dream lineup of musicians—ex-Quiet Riot guitarist Randy Rhoads, Rainbow bassist Bob Daisley, and sometime Uriah Heep drummer Lee Kerslake. Rhoads, a twenty-four-year-old virtuoso, possessed skills as a lead guitarist that were matched only by his Californian colleague Eddie Van Halen. He had been recruited to the band with an audition that has since become the stuff of rock legend. Apparently he had simply arrived at a Los Angeles studio with a Gibson Les Paul and a Fender amp; on tuning his guitar and warming up for five minutes, he was told that he'd got the job.

Check out the songs "I Don't Know" and "Crazy Train," both career classics for Ozzy;

BELOW: Live at Last *was the first live album by Black Sabbath. It was released without the band's knowledge and is considered something of an unofficial bootleg in some circles.*

ABOVE: *Ozzy's first solo tour in support of* Blizzard of Ozz, *photographed here at the Hammersmith Odeon with guitarist Randy Rhoads, bassist Bob Daisley, and drummer Lee Kerslake.*

ABOVE: Blizzard of Ozz *was Ozzy's first solo album release and proved that the former Sabbath singer could make it on his own.* **RIGHT:** *Ozzy and Lee Kerslake photographed at Port Vale in 1981.*

"Mr. Crowley," featuring an awe-inspiring organ intro from the great Rick Wakeman, harks back to Sabbath's early Satanic image, based as it is on the story of the eccentric English occultist Aleister Crowley. It's mainstream stuff, despite Ozzy's supposedly spooky image, and it's jammed full of memorable hooks and incredible solos from Rhoads. Little wonder the album performed well: as the late Motörhead front man Lemmy told me, "I thought Ozzy's first solo album was better than all of Black Sabbath's albums put together."

The battle between Sabbath and Ozzy—inasmuch as there was one, since the friendships between the two parties would tentatively resume within a few years—wasn't over. In 1981, Sabbath scheduled the recording of a second LP with Ronnie James

Dio, this time featuring Appice on drums. *The Mob Rules* was scheduled for release in the autumn, after another huge tour in the summer. As Appice recalled, "After a month or two off, they were like, 'We're gonna start rehearsing for a new album, and we're gonna call it *The Mob Rules*.' Tony and Geezer lived in California, so we rehearsed it in L.A. We started jamming in the studio, because that's the way the band writes all the time. They just set up the studio, Tony or Geezer will start playing, and I'll just play, and I recorded everything. I was in charge of the tapes; I still have tapes of this stuff.

"We'd come in the next day and listen to some of the riffs; everybody would choose the riffs and we'd start building a song on that. That's how we did it. Then we went into this studio called Can-Am in the San Fernando Valley here to record. They were gonna invest in the studio, but when we went in they didn't like it. So we moved over to the Record Plant in L.A. and did the rest of the album there."

Expectations were high when, on October 11, 1981, *The Mob Rules* was released. Its title track, which also features on the soundtrack for the cult Canadian film *Heavy Metal*, is a solid enough effort, but the rest of the album doesn't quite match up to *Heaven and Hell*— unfortunately for Sabbath, who now faced the ignominy of being outstripped by the specter

LEFT: *Singer Ronnie James Dio fronting Sabbath during the 1980 tour, photographed here at the Hammersmith Odeon in January.* **ABOVE:** *Sabbath's answer to Blizzard of Ozz was 1981's* The Mob Rules, *the band's tenth studio album and the first without Bill Ward on the drums.*

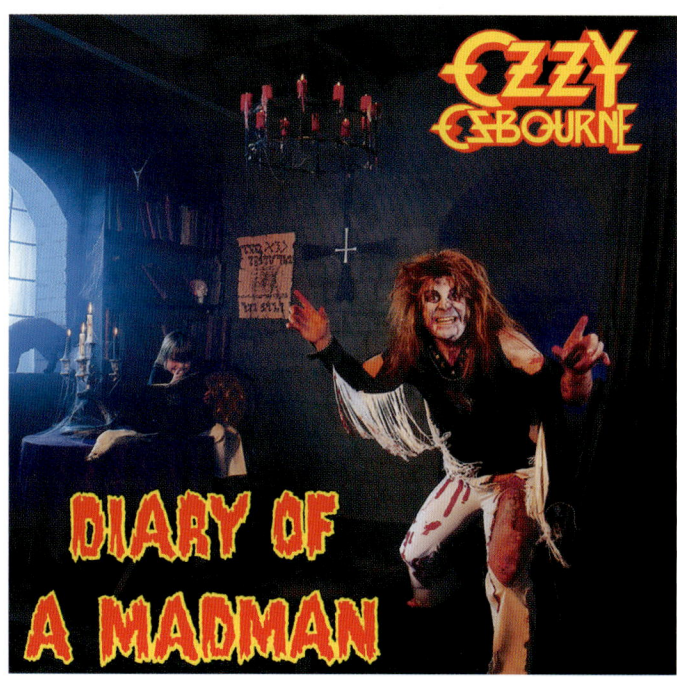

of its former singer. Ozzy's second solo LP, *Diary of a Madman*, appeared on November 7 and capitalized on its maker's rapidly rising profile as a true rock nutter: a man who walked the walk with full commitment. Take for example the rumor that Ozzy had enlivened a 1981 meeting with his new record company, CBS, by biting off the head of a live dove—a rumor that turned out to be true. "You Can't Kill Rock 'n' Roll," a song from the new LP, bore its title for good reason.

The *Madman* theme was rapidly translating into reality, as anyone who witnessed Ozzy's tour through Europe with Saxon in support that year will know. It became known as the "Night of the Living Dead" tour among journalists, thanks to incidents involving a collapsing crane, trucks breaking down, and other, more shocking elements, such as Ozzy's decision to throw raw meat into the

OPPOSITE: *Dio photographed at the Hammersmith Odeon in January 1980.*
ABOVE LEFT: *Ozzy's answer to* The Mob Rules *was his second solo album,* Diary of a Madman*, which "capitalized on its maker's rapidly rising profile as a true rock nutter."*
ABOVE: *Ozzy and his son, Louis, during the photoshoot for* Diary of a Madman*.*

audience. After dates at which he treated the crowd to helpings of calves' liver and pigs' intestines, audience members began to bring their own offal to throw back at him. This rapidly escalated until, after a while, Ozzy was reportedly being showered with live frogs, snakes, and even cats.

At a show in Des Moines, Iowa, on January 20, 1982, a fan threw a live bat onto Ozzy's stage. The singer picked it up and, assuming it was made of rubber, bit off its head. This necessitated a series of anti-rabies injections into his stomach after the show, and led to several decades' worth of bat-themed jokes, not to mention a reputation for mental derangement.

OPPOSITE TOP: *Ozzy and bassist Randy Rhoads in Los Angeles in 1981.* **OPPOSITE BOTTOM:** *Ozzy promoting his second solo album,* Diary of a Madman, *in Los Angeles in 1981.* **ABOVE:** *Ozzy's band,* Blizzard of Ozz, *photographed in Oakland in 1981; from left: Rudy Sarzo, Randy Rhoads, Tommy Aldridge, and Ozzy Osbourne.*

Ozzy improved on this by inadvertently annoying the entire American South the following month when he urinated on the Alamo Cenotaph in San Antonio, Texas. An eighteenth-century building designated as a National Historic Landmark, the monument was and still is sacred to many patriotic Texans. Ozzy's decision to bless it with his bodily fluids didn't win him many friends.

Soon afterward, when the glam-metal band Mötley Crüe—whose members were also no strangers to drugs, booze, and antisocial behavior—toured with Ozzy, they witnessed yet more curious, not to say life-threatening, antics on his part. As Crüe bassist Nikki Sixx recalls in the band's 2001 autobiography, *The Dirt*, Ozzy once snorted a line of ants off the ground next to a hotel swimming-pool, urinated on the ground, and then licked it up—and then, after demanding that Sixx do the same, licked up *his* pool of urine, too.

As I said earlier, you really couldn't make this stuff up.

5

REBIRTH AND DEATH

1982–1983

The madness continued into 1982—a year of tragedy for the current and former members of Black Sabbath. In January, the Dio–Iommi–Butler–Appice lineup toured the UK and US, although several shows had to be postponed after Iommi's father died.

A couple of months later, Ozzy Osbourne—touring with Randy Rhoads, Rudy Sarzo, and Tommy Aldridge—was on his own tour of the States. On March 19, Ozzy and his band were traveling to a show in Orlando, Florida, from Knoxville, Tennessee. The tour bus needed some repairs, so the driver, Andrew Aycock, stopped in the Florida town of Leesburg, where he owned a house. While repairs were underway, Ozzy took a nap in the bus and Aycock invited keyboardist Don Airey and tour manager Jake Duncan for a spin in the small Beechcraft Bonanza airplane he kept at his home.

OPPOSITE: *Geezer Butler and Tony Iommi, the only remaining two original members of Black Sabbath, in 1983.*

ABOVE: *Ozzy Osbourne and Randy Rhoads at a concert in Rosemont, Illinois, in January 1982. Rhoads would die in a plane crash a couple of months later.*

On their return, Aycock took Rhoads and Ozzy's tour seamstress, Rachael Youngblood, for a second flight. Sarzo later recalled that although Rhoads was afraid of flying, he was a keen photographer and wanted to attempt some aerial shots from the plane. He asked Aldridge to accompany him, but the drummer refused, explaining that he thought it might be dangerous, as Aycock had been driving the bus all night. Later, Ozzy stated that, had he been awake at that time, he would have joined Rhoads on the plane.

After a few minutes in the air, Aycock decided to put the plane into a shallow dive toward the tour bus, but he misjudged the angle of the dive. Pulling up too late, he clipped the bus at about five feet from the ground with the aircraft's left wing. Because it was executing a left bank at the time, the body of the plane passed over the top of the bus. It then flipped over and hit a large pine tree, severing the trunk about ten feet above the ground.

A fraction of a second later, the plane crashed directly into the garage of the

Georgian-style mansion situated about sixty feet from the bus, in which two cars were parked. The fuel tanks ignited on impact, and the plane and garage were engulfed in a fireball. Rhoads, Youngblood, and Aycock were killed instantly.

The shock of the incident was immense: to this day, the singer calls this date the worst day of his life. In the aftermath, Sharon organized a replacement guitarist to take Rhoads's place in order to complete the tour and prevent Ozzy from having a breakdown. Ex-Gillan guitarist Bernie Tormé was recruited a few days later, before being replaced himself after seven shows by Brad Gillis of Night Ranger.

ABOVE: *Sabbath released* Live Evil, *the band's second live album, in 1982.* **BELOW:** *As rumors swirled that Ronnie James Dio was quitting Sabbath, it was believed that singer David Coverdale, formerly of Deep Purple, would be joining the band; he denied the possibility.*

LIVE EVIL

Meanwhile, Black Sabbath was winding up the *Mob Rules* tour, which crossed the United States and Canada once again in the early summer. Perhaps because Ronnie James Dio was working his way toward quitting the band, a popular rumor had it that at some stage that summer, the singer David Coverdale—once of Deep Purple's Mk. III lineup, and at the time in the middle of a successful thirteen-year run with Whitesnake—was asked to join Sabbath. He told me that this was never a possibility, though, saying, "I could never see myself singing Ozzy's songs."

Ozzy and Sharon were married in July '82, cementing a partnership that continues to this day despite regular divorce rumors: as his manager, bringing the singer out of the depression that followed Rhoads's death must have been just as a great a challenge for Sharon as the one that came when he was ejected from Black Sabbath three years previously. A live album of Sabbath songs, *Speak of the Devil*, was released the same month: this completed both Ozzy's management deal with Don Arden and his contract with Arden's Jet label.

Sabbath was also releasing a live album,

BELOW: *Ozzy and his manager, Sharon Arden, married on July 7, 1982, on Maui, Hawaii.*

the Americans and the British. But I tried not to let that happen: we always had two limos, for example, and rather than always get in the limo with Ronnie I would get in the limo with Geezer. I had no problems with anybody—I was having a good time—and Tony and Geezer had no problems with me; it was just with Ronnie. It was a lot of egos."

The differences of opinion sometimes got serious, as the drummer remembered. "There were a couple of fights backstage with Tony and Ronnie screaming at each other.

ABOVE: *In 1982, Ozzy released a live album of Sabbath songs,* Speak of the Devil, *completing his management deal with Don Arden and his contract with Arden's label.* **BELOW:** *A close-up of Dio performing with Black Sabbath at New York's Madison Square Garden.*

the tiresomely titled *Live Evil* (not to be confused with *Live-Evil*, a 1971 LP by Miles Davis). By now, Sabbath was beginning to find themselves slightly on the outside of modern heavy metal; in the early '80s, thrash metal was on the way toward the dominance it would achieve later in the decade, spearheaded by Metallica and Slayer and a host of lesser-ran bands such as Exciter, which supported Sabbath in Canada that year. Black Sabbath's gradual descent from the top of the heavy metal tree began here, when Dio quit after the release of the live LP.

Vinny Appice saw the parting of the ways firsthand. As he told me, "I don't think anything really started to go downhill until the live album. I mean, I got along with everybody. I love Tony. He's a practical joker and so am I, and Geezer was cool. But the only problem was toward the end when we were recording the live album—the relationships between Tony and Ronnie, and Geezer and Ronnie, were starting to go downhill. It became like

Two hotheaded Italians! I don't know what they were arguing about—I would just say, whoa, and not get involved with any of it. So by the end of the tour you could feel the vibe between them. . . ."

Appice speculated that the mix of *Live Evil* may have been the final straw. "What happened was, during the mix of the live album, they booked the studio for two o'clock. But they wouldn't get there until four or five o'clock, and this was an expensive studio. Me and Ronnie would be there at two. You tell me two, I'm there. So are we gonna sit around for three or four hours? So, we'd start working on the stuff and then they'd show up and it caused a problem because we'd say, we've worked on the drum sound a little bit. And I guess Tony and Geezer didn't want to do it that way.

"They don't communicate: when there's a problem, there's no confrontation. Tony doesn't like confrontation, he goes through someone else. When Tony doesn't talk to you, you know there's a problem. You can't go to Tony unless you really sit down and talk. He'd talk to me once in a while. You know, I never had a problem with these guys—I love these guys. They had a problem with Ronnie.

"I had no say in this; I just came in when they wanted me in. But Ronnie wanted to do some work, so he would start doing whatever needed to be done, and they took that as

LEFT: *Dio, Iommi, Butler, and Appice performing at New York's Madison Square Garden just months before the departure of Dio and Appice.*

Ronnie sneaking in the studio and doing stuff behind their back. And they might have left and gone to the pub . . . well, Ronnie's there, he's a workaholic. Yeah, I'm an innocent party. I'm not gonna say, well, I'm not going in until they go in! I was just a little kid going hey, I'm having a good time—stop fighting, guys!"

When the end came, it came quickly. "Eventually they accused us of going in the studio and doing stuff behind their back," Appice continued, "[which] was a little unjust, because I didn't really have any say in the mixing. Maybe I'd say to [producer] Martin Birch that the drums needed a little more bottom end here and there, but I wasn't gonna say that the guitars were too low or whatever. So if Ronnie said, 'Let's go in at five today,' I'd say okay, because we were driving into the studio from the same area anyway.

"But then Ronnie said, 'I'm leaving Sabbath and I'm going to start my own band—do you want to do it with me?' I said yeah. I could relate to Ronnie at that point a little bit more than with Tony and Geezer, and I thought it would be cool to be in a new band, having had a lot of success with Sabbath. It would be fun to build something up from the beginning. But I think they still wanted me to play with them."

ENTER GILLAN

Dio and Appice left Black Sabbath in October 1982: the pair went on to form the very successful Dio, leaving Tony Iommi and Geezer Butler behind. However, a night in the pub early the next year led to a remarkable,

if short-lived, new lineup. Sometime Deep Purple singer and then solo artist Ian Gillan was the new singer, perhaps improbably: although Purple and Sabbath had co-existed in a state of more or less mutual respect for a decade and more at this point, the two group's images were dissimilar, to say the least.

> ## "By the time we did *Born Again*, I was in my tenth or twelfth attempt at being sober . . ."
>
> —BILL WARD

Gillan joined the band in a state of serious intoxication, he later revealed, having forgotten to inform his manager that he was joining what was jocularly referred to as "Purple Sabbath" until the morning after the fateful night. Still, as Butler told me, "We'd finished with the Ronnie version of the band, and I said to Tony, 'It's getting to be a bit of a joke calling it Sabbath, isn't it?' And he totally agreed. I think the management at the time suggested getting Ian and calling it a Gillan–Iommi–Butler–Ward album, not a Black Sabbath album, which was the way we and Gillan felt. We just thought it would be an interesting thing to do as a one-off."

Before rehearsals could begin, a drummer was needed. A call was placed to Bill Ward, who was on his way toward sobriety by the end of 1982. As he told me, "By the time we did *Born Again*, I was in my tenth or twelfth attempt at being sober: when we did it I was completely stark-staring sober." However,

ABOVE: *Ian Gillan, formerly a solo artist and Deep Purple singer, joined Black Sabbath in 1982, replacing Ronnie James Dio.*

although Ward played well during the recording of the *Born Again* album, he fell off the wagon when it was finished and informed the band that he couldn't do the subsequent tour.

"It's a physical illness," he continued. "It's a killer, there's no doubt about that. There's a dependency, but it's a mental illness—a spiritual malady—and then there's the physical illness that comes along with it. It's not a question of saying, 'Oh, fuck it, I'm gonna turn my life around and start over, I'm gonna pull my socks up here and fight this

thing called alcoholism': every time you try to fight it, it wins. It's very powerful and an absolutely deadly illness."

Ward was also suffering from clinical depression. "I didn't know at the time that I was in maudlin depression. I didn't know at the time that I was feeling so sorry for myself, which is a shit place to be. At that time it was mental depression: there was probably some clinical depression as well, but there was no medication at the time. I'd already tried and failed to be sober, and I couldn't stand

drinking any more, so there was no place to live any more."

He briefly considered suicide, but when it came down to it and he had a gun pointed at his own head, something prevented him from taking the final step. "I couldn't pull the trigger," he said. "I tried to kill myself three times. And I didn't have the balls to pull the trigger, so I had no choice. I had to get sober. And I didn't want to be sober: I wanted to be dead. And of course I failed miserably, thank God, and I couldn't do the booze any more. I just couldn't do it. So I chose to be sober, and it wasn't easy. It wasn't easy at all."

Sabbath duly asked Bev Bevan, the drummer in the Electric Light Orchestra, to step in for the *Born Again* tour. On September 24, 1983, *Born Again* itself was released and went to No. 4 in the UK. Oddly, the album came out under the name Black

Sabbath, although this clearly had not been the band's intention.

Butler told me, "*Born Again* wasn't supposed to be a Sabbath album. That's where the record company [Vertigo] betrayed us again . . . we finished it and gave it to the record company, who said, 'We've paid for a Sabbath album and that's what we're putting it out as.' There was nothing we could do about it. There's some good songs on it, but the production's really bad. We were still trying to do the mixing ourselves instead of getting a good mixing person in."

Gillan enjoyed the Black Sabbath experience. "It was great fun," he told me. "It was definitely a short-term thing. It came

ABOVE: *Born Again, released in 1983, was the band's eleventh studio album and only one with lead vocalist Ian Gillan. Bill Ward returned to Sabbath to record the album but could not do the subsequent tour.* **BELOW:** *Black Sabbath at a signing at Tower Records with Ian Gillan.* **OPPOSITE:** *The* Born Again *tour kicked off with Bev Bevan as the drummer, together with Ian Gillan, Tony Iommi, and Geezer Butler, seen here in 1983.*

about in a most bizarre fashion: we just got drunk and that was it, and I was in the band before I knew it—quite happily and without any regrets too, I might say. We had to complete the whole album, and we had to rehearse, and as usual I had to do a lot of catch-up writing. I didn't see a lot of the band because they were night people and I was really a day person. They'd be coming home from the clubs in Birmingham as I was getting up and cooking my breakfast.

"Anyone can produce the most amazing heavy-rock sounds with today's machines, but it's not the chords—it's how you play them," he added. "It's the person that counts. That was very important. If you ever talk about tracing things back to their roots—if ever I could see a direct line from Seattle to Birmingham, it would be Tony Iommi, right back at the birth of it. I never saw anyone else play like him back in those days. No, not better than Ritchie: how could he be better? It's like the rock Olympics: who can play or shout or drum faster or louder? It's a ludicrous concept in my book. They are what they are—neither is better than the other."

The ensuing tour became infamous thanks to the extravagant stage set—a replica of the Stonehenge columns—and the movie *Spinal Tap*, which lampooned it mercilessly the following year. The columns were fifteen

meters in height rather than the intended fifteen feet, and they barely fit into some of the venues on the tour—if at all.

THE END IS NIGH

On December 10, 1983, Ozzy Osbourne released a new album, *Bark at the Moon*, another excellent, melodic rock LP that cemented his position as madman of metal, although he too was finding it a little difficult to maintain a foothold in the modern rock landscape. At least he had a full band, though: over in the Sabbath camp, Gillan quit to rejoin the reformed Deep Purple and Ward—finally sober—retook his drum stool from Bev Bevan.

In May 1984, Iommi selected a singer called David Donato who had sung in the

OPPOSITE: *Ian Gillan and Tony Iommi performing at the Reading Festival in 1983.* RIGHT: Bark at the Moon *was Ozzy Osbourne's third studio album and the first since a plane crash in 1982 forced changes in Ozzy's band.*

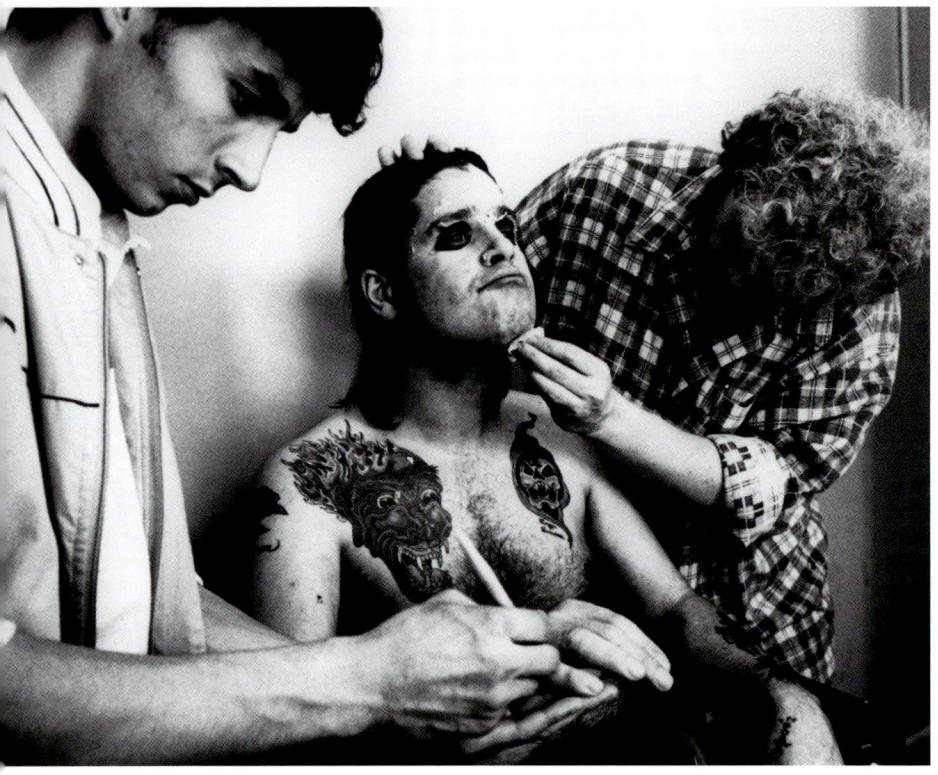

supportive. They knew. I said, 'I just can't do it.' There were so many times after that I wanted to go back and play with them, I just felt terrible. I just wanted to play music with the guys that I'd been playing with all my life, but the reason I couldn't go back was that I knew that things would be the same again, with someone else."

To make things worse, Geezer Butler had also quit to form his own band, leaving Tony Iommi as the last man in Black Sabbath. Could this be the end?

LEFT: *Makeup being put on Ozzy for the* Bark at the Moon *photoshoot in 1983.* BELOW: *An outtake from the* Bark at the Moon *photoshoot, featuring Ozzy dressed as a werewolf.*

glam-metal band White Tiger, among other acts. Donato, a former model, had worked with Keith Relf of the Yardbirds and other respected musicians, but neither he nor a singer called Ron Keel stayed in the band for long. Ward also took off after only a year or so back in the band, uncertain of Sabbath's future in the post-Ozzy era.

"I had the same feelings that I'd had when Ronnie and Ian were in the band," he told me, "which was basically that it didn't feel the same as it had with Ozzy. I would have loved to continue, but it felt that I was being dishonest with myself. So I said my goodbyes. After that I basically knew that there was no way back. And it was at that time that I decided—by my own truths—that I couldn't do Sabbath without Ozz. They were really

ABOVE: *Ozzy and the Bark at the Moon–era band at Ridge Farm Studios in 1983.*

6

SEVENTH SONS

1984–1990

Themed award-winning musical *Jesus Christ Superstar* might be an unlikely source for a Black Sabbath singer, but by 1984, options weren't exactly thick on the ground for Tony Iommi. Plucked from the title role for an audition, Ohio native Jeff Fenholt—the subject of much discussion among Black Sabbath fans ever since, largely because at one point Iommi denied even knowing him—scored highly for his vocals but never formally signed with the band, according to new drummer Eric Singer. The audition took place in early 1985, with Fenholt assisting on demo material for a potential solo album by Iommi plus session men Singer and bassist Gordon Copley from the Lita Ford Band.

By May 1985, Sabbath was back to Iommi and Singer (himself a new arrival via Lita Ford's backing band). This sorry state of affairs was

OPPOSITE: *Sabbath's early 1986 lineup included Dave Spitz, Eric Singer, Glenn Hughes, Tony Iommi, and Geoff Nicholls.* ABOVE: *Jeff Fenholt as the title character in* Jesus Christ Superstar *has been the subject of much discussion among Sabbath fans.*

Black Sabbath temporarily reunited for the Live Aid concert on July 13, 1985, where the original four members played a three-song set. Ozzy (above) and Iommi (left) had difficulty working together and rumors of a full reunion were soon quashed.

overshadowed, at least temporarily, by the Live Aid concert on July 13 the same year, for which the original foursome of Ozzy, Iommi, Butler, and Ward made a one-off appearance together at JFK Stadium in Philadelphia. Take a look at the performance on YouTube: you'll see Black Sabbath kicking off their three-song, fifteen-minute set with a version of "Children of the Grave." Note the spandex, mirrored shades, and lack of chemistry between the musicians: everything points to a fairly uninspired collaboration. "Iron Man" and "Paranoid" were delivered with more conviction, although any possibility of a full reunion was soon quashed.

As Butler later explained, legal issues between Don Arden and his daughter Sharon were an obstruction. "Ozzy was served with lawsuit papers from his father-in-law," he said. "He took it personally from Tony, even though Tony didn't have anything to do with it."

It was back to work, then, for Iommi, whose concept for a solo album—which he wanted to call *Seventh Star*—had extended as far to bass and drum tracks, laid down during the

Fenholt sessions. He still required a front man, however, so he called Glenn Hughes, the singer and bassist whose unearthly vocals had graced albums by Trapeze, Deep Purple, and a host of other heavy rock projects since the late 1960s, all of which earned him the nickname "The Voice of Rock."

Once on board, Hughes recorded his vocals at Cherokee Studios in Hollywood in July and August. Lyrics came variously from keyboardist Geoff Nicholls, producer Jeff Glixman, and Hughes himself. Iommi added a

BELOW: *Ozzy, Sharon, and their babies (from left) Jack, Kelly, and Aimee, photographed at their home in England in 1986.*

bassist, Dave Spitz—nicknamed "The Beast" for his Wookiee-like head and body hair—and the new lineup was ready to tour.

When *Seventh Star* was released on March 1, 1986, it was billed as "Black Sabbath Featuring Tony Iommi"—a bizarre compromise to which Iommi had been forced to agree by his record label. Hughes later recalled, "For me, the album, when we recorded it, was called 'Tony Iommi,' period. But when it was all mixed his manager said, 'Let's call it Black Sabbath!' to make more money. If you listen to it as a Tony Iommi album, it's great. If you

listen to it as a Black Sabbath album, it's not very good. Let's just say that I don't belong in Black Sabbath. I've said that all along."

Hughes was right. Accustomed to playing bass while singing, he was a little lost onstage with only a mic to hold. In poor shape after years of drug abuse, his confidence was low. Worst of all, a pre-tour scuffle robbed him of his golden voice, as he told me some years ago.

"What happened was, three days before pre-production, we were in this massive studio where everybody plays showcases," he said. "The night before, my girlfriend's mother

had flown in. I'd never met her before, and she turned out to be Satan's child from hell. She was a nightmare. We had a big argument and she pulled a gun. This was the kind of person I used to hang out with before I got sober. We were pretty drunk and [Sabbath tour manager] John Downey, who is now deceased, got into a bit of a thing with me, and hit me.

"I probably provoked him verbally," Hughes continued. "He took it on himself to hit the lead singer of a band that was going on tour tomorrow. Even Don Arden said to him, 'Couldn't you have hit him in the back or something?' He really, really hit me—so hard that the bottom part of my eye socket was fractured—not known to me—and it went into my nose, which caused clots of blood to gather on my larynx. Over a period of days it kept building up and closed the air off, so I was making kind of a reedy sound. On my fifth gig with Sabbath in Worcester, Massachusetts, I couldn't sing, even after a month of rehearsals with Tony and the guys where I sounded great."

Hughes couldn't sing the notes required, and he knew that Iommi and Arden would not be happy. "I couldn't physically sing because of the injury," he sighed. "I'd never been on stage before in my whole career and not been

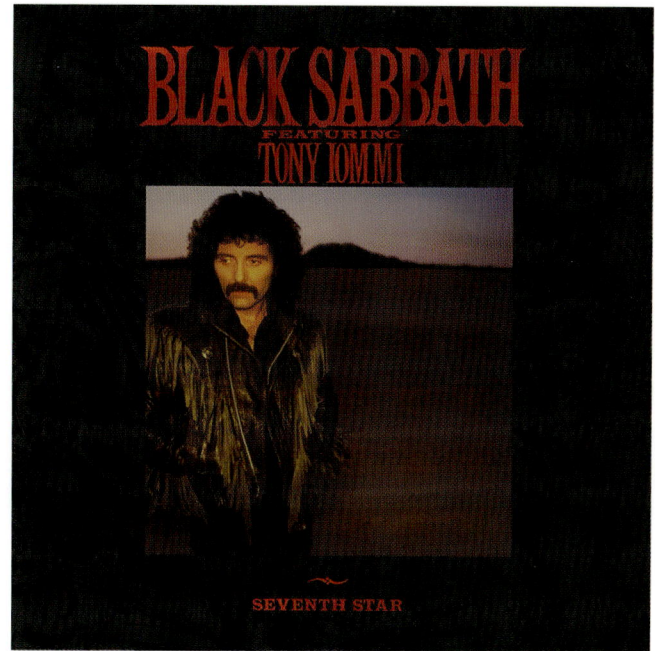

OPPOSITE: *Sabbath's 1985 lineup, featuring Geoff Nicholls, Tony Iommi, Dave Spitz, Eric Singer, and Glenn Hughes.*
ABOVE: Seventh Star *was Black Sabbath's twelfth studio album; it was awkwardly billed as "Black Sabbath Featuring Tony Iommi," a bizarre arrangement.*

able to sing. I didn't know what the problem was. I knew I'd been hit in the face, but can you imagine being this great, talented 'Voice of Rock' and not being able to sing? It was the worst nightmare for me."

Iommi wasted no time in ousting Hughes: these days, however, the singer is relaxed about the incident, having been fit and drug-free since 1997. "I wasn't kicked out, or asked to leave the band because I was getting high," he reasoned. "It was just an unfortunate thing that happened, and it was God's intervention as well. I wasn't supposed to be on stage doing those things, and I was clearly not well. The worst things that happen in a person's life turn out to be great. Everyone in life that I've met has had a dark period, and this was mine."

The two men ultimately rebuilt their friendship. As Iommi later explained,

"She was a nightmare. We had a big argument and she pulled a gun . . . "

—GLENN HUGHES

"*Seventh Star* was not supposed to be a Black Sabbath album. Glenn thought, and I thought, that he was singing the vocals for what was supposed to be my first solo album. When the record company insisted I release it as a Black Sabbath album, we had to go on tour as Black Sabbath, and that's not something Glenn wanted to do, or even thought he'd have to do. He's a great singer, but he's not a Black Sabbath singer, as those few gigs we did with him proved. It also didn't help that Glenn was in a very bad place personally at that time. He was heavily into drugs and alcohol, and he was constantly surrounded by drug dealers and all sorts of shady characters."

NUMBER NINE, NUMBER NINE . . .

Sabbath's ninth singer in seven years was Ray Gillen, a twenty-five-year-old New Jersey resident whose biggest exposure before this point had been with Rondinelli, the project

ABOVE: *Ray Gillen, photographed here in 1986, was Sabbath's ninth singer in seven years.* BELOW: *On April 11, 1986, Sabbath, fronted by Ray Gillen, played at the Nassau Coliseum in Uniondale, New York.*

of ex-Rainbow drummer Bobby Rondinelli. Gillen—not to be confused with Ian Gillan, of course—arrived before Hughes's departure and debuted on March 29 in New Haven. The audience seemed to accept the new recruit, and both band and management breathed a collective sigh of relief.

Replacing Dave Spitz with veteran bassist Bob Daisley, Sabbath checked into Air Studios in Montserrat for pre-production on another new album. Jeff Glixman was scheduled to produce, and Gillen settled into Iommi's working pattern with apparent ease. The LP, titled *The Eternal Idol*, was completed toward the end of 1986, and was scheduled to appear in mid-1987. Questions circled about whether it could reverse the downward spiral for Sabbath.

Meanwhile, Ozzy Osbourne was promoting his own new album, *The Ultimate Sin*—his fourth in six years. Released on

ABOVE: *Toward the end of 1986, Sabbath gathered at Air Studios in Montserrat for production on another album,* **The Eternal Idol. BELOW:** *In 1986, Ozzy released his fourth studio album in six years,* **The Ultimate Sin.** *It reestablished him as a force in metal music.*

February 22, 1986, the LP reestablished the Ozzy brand after the moderately successful post–Randy Rhoads album *Bark at the Moon*, released three years before. The extensive *Ultimate Sin* tour—spanning March to August 1986, and featuring the up-and-coming Metallica in support—grossed vast sums and brought Ozzy back to the top of the metal tree in commercial terms.

Combining forces with Metallica—then at a critical commercial peak with their career-best *Master of Puppets* album—was an expert move. Thrash metal fans came to the shows in droves, ready to be converted to the Ozzy cause, while established fans were shown that

he and his wife Sharon still had their fingers on the commercial pulse.

The Ultimate Sin was an unashamedly radio-friendly album, complete with a front-cover caricature of Ozzy as a demon from the ninth circle of hell, accompanied by an unidentified

female figure. Jake E. Lee appeared on guitar, while a new rhythm section of Phil Soussan on bass, Randy Castillo on drums, and Mike Moran on keyboards performed a set of moderately interesting songs which, rather like *Seventh Star*, were popular among fans of melodic rock.

The high point of the album was undoubtedly "Shot in the Dark," a Top 20 single in February 1986. The video for this song is an '80s classic, inspiring both hilarity and nostalgia among fans to this day. Thanks to Ozzy's ludicrous costume, hammy acting, and out-of-shape physique, it's impossible to take it seriously.

BELOW: *Ozzy and guitarist Jake E. Lee playing in New York City in 1986 during the extensive* Ultimate Sin *tour.* **RIGHT:** *Metallica, fronted by James Hetfield, opened for Ozzy's band during the* Ultimate Sin *tour.*

PARENTAL ADVISORY

Less amusing developments were in store for Ozzy in 1986. One of his old songs, "Suicide Solution," was in the news thanks to a trial in which the family of a youth named John McCollum, who had committed suicide while listening to the song, hired an organization called the Institute for Bio-Acoustics Research (IBAR) to assess its content. IBAR claimed to have located subliminal lyrics in the song, recorded 60 percent faster than the normal rate of speech and "audible enough that their meaning and true intent becomes clear after being listened to over and over again." The lyrics were said to be, "Why try, why try? Get the gun and try it! Shoot, shoot, shoot,"

followed by laughter. All of this was dismissed by the court, but it led to much press attention on the subject.

All of this tied in regrettably with the so-called "Satanic Panic" that plagued the American record industry in the mid-'80s. Readers will recall the Parents' Music Resource Center (PMRC). Formed by Mary "Tipper" Gore, wife of Bill Clinton's future vice president, Al Gore, plus some of the bored wives of prominent Washington politicians and businessmen, the aim of this pressure group was to persuade the US recording industry to censor itself in order to protect minors from the more extreme music of the day.

As it happens, the idea of the public

ABOVE: *James McCollum Sr., father of a youth who committed suicide while listening to Ozzy's "Suicide Solution," photographed with a copy of Ozzy's* Speak of the Devil.

policing its own activities is not new; any society needs to regulate itself. But what was slightly sinister about the PMRC was that it presented an agenda that crushed anything and everything that was missing from its "approved" list. This included a lot of heavy metal, but it also meant that the freedom of speech of many mainstream pop and rock artists was also compromised.

To most reasonable observers' surprise, rather than telling Tipper and her cronies to disappear back to the Washington golf clubs from whence they came, the Recording Industry Association of America (RIAA) bowed to the PMRC's demands and introduced the infamous "Parental Advisory" stickers that adorn CDs to this day.

The PMRC then muscled its way into all sectors of the entertainment industry, beginning with TV and radio—the most potent disseminators of "undesirable" music to the masses. After being told of the PMRC's concerns over rock lyrics, Eddie Fritts, the boss of the National Association of Broadcasters, contacted the staff of forty-five record labels, requesting that lyric sheets accompany all songs scheduled for radio airplay. The most famous recipient of legal action in this time was probably Ozzy, whose early material was obviously the stuff of nightmares for the PMRC.

Perhaps "the people" were looking for something new to alleviate the pressures of daily life, just as Ozzy did with his (now-reduced) alcohol habit? If so, this lay just around the corner—in the form of music which would make Ozzy's songs, and indeed those of Black Sabbath, seem as offensive as a Christmas cracker.

This was thrash metal, the first incarnation of the "extreme metal" wave that later partitioned into black, death, and doom metal subgenres alongside an extreme form of punk rock called grindcore. By the early-to-mid 1990s, these forms of metal had their own, recognizable features, but back in the mid-'80s, extreme metal basically meant faster, angrier, more aggressive, and occasionally more technical music than the traditional heavy metal sounds offered by Sabbath.

All this meant that Black Sabbath was about to enter a period of deep unfashionability. Struggling to find a permanent, credible singer after post-Dio experiments with Ian Gillan, Glenn Hughes, and Ray Gillen, who left before the release of Sabbath's 1987 album *The Eternal Idol*, Iommi was at a low point in his career.

Meanwhile, it had been a busy couple of years for Ozzy, whose move into the realm of melodic rock had proven to be a commercially savvy decision. He had become something of a mainstream success—"mainstream" here meaning that metal fans liked him, but the nonmetal press still had no idea who he was—thanks to two successful LPs, *The Ultimate Sin* and *Tribute*. A high point of the former was "Killer of Giants," an anti–nuclear weapons anthem over acoustic chords; the latter, a live LP of the Randy Rhoads lineup recorded at its peak in 1981 and issued on May 23, 1987, was excellent, consisting of songs from *Blizzard of*

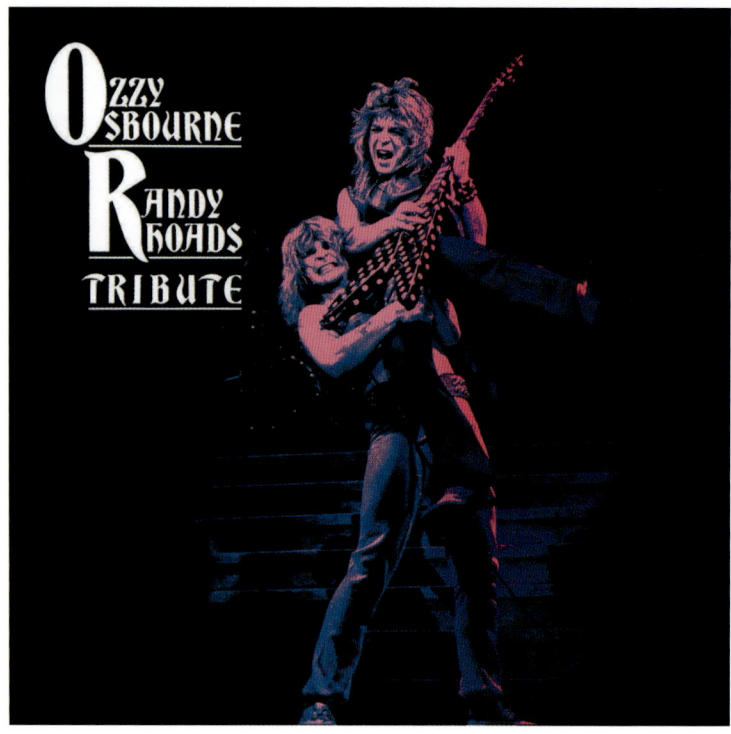

A summer 1987 tour was booked while Martin laid down new vocal tracks for *The Eternal Idol*. Sabbath flew to Greece and then to South Africa for festival shows at Sun City, causing some protests from anti-apartheid groups: as Bevan refused to play these dates, a session drummer called Terry Chimes—formerly of The Clash—temporarily took over.

The Eternal Idol was released on November 28, 1987, and contains some high-quality songs—"Nightmare," with its *Tubular Bells*–style keyboard intro; the instrumental "Scarlet Pimpernel"; and the title track itself. It's no *Sabbath Bloody Sabbath*, of course, and it only reached No. 66 in the UK, staying on the chart for one week—a sign of the times as much as of the music's quality.

The *Eternal Idol* tour, a jaunt through Germany, Italy, and Holland in November and December 1987, featured a new bassist. Dave

Ozz and *Diary of a Madman* and some Sabbath classics—"Children of the Grave" and the obvious "Paranoid" and "Iron Man."

All of this activity meant that Ozzy's star was in the ascendant throughout this period, although his old band could not say the same. Dave Spitz, Eric Singer, and Ray Gillen all parted ways with Iommi at this point: sadly, Gillen's career was later cut short by his premature death from AIDS in 1993, at only thirty-three years old. Iommi, once again left only with long-term musical partner Geoff Nicholls (the longest-serving band member outside the original quartet), recruited a whole new band to complete the *Eternal Idol* album. His new singer was the golden-larynxed Tony Martin, whose manager had worked with Sabbath in previous years; Bev Bevan played drums and Dave Spitz returned to bass duties.

Spitz had left the band again before the tour, requiring Iommi to recruit session man Jo Burt, who had worked with Freddie Mercury. Terry Chimes remained aboard as drummer, making this incarnation of Sabbath one of the oddest to date.

Essentially, 1987 was Black Sabbath's worst year yet, despite Iommi's dogged attempts to keep the band alive. The band also ended its deal with the Vertigo label, signing instead with IRS Records, the American company founded by Police and Sting manager Miles Copeland. Iommi wasn't about to give up, though: a new lineup, featuring the two Tonys, Blue Murder drummer Cozy Powell, and session bassist Laurence Cottle (who had worked with Eric Clapton, Brian Eno, and Powell, among others) gathered in August 1988 to rehearse for a new album, titled *Headless Cross*.

GOING WYLDE

Ozzy had a new band, too, or at least a new guitar player. Jake E. Lee's replacement was the remarkable Zakk Wylde (real name Jeffrey Wielandt), a previously unknown hotshot who ended up as his longest-serving axe-man. Wylde's incendiary playing on the new album, *No Rest for the Wicked*, helped to make it one of Ozzy's best in some time.

Wylde went on to create an uncompromising persona, especially since the formation of his own band, Black Label Society. As he told me, "I gotta keep it simple, like a caveman. All I do in my life is make sure I have massive sex

OPPOSITE TOP: *Ozzy's live album* Tribute *featured his work with Randy Rhoads who died in 1982.* OPPOSITE BOTTOM: *Sabbath's thirteenth album,* Eternal Idol, *was finally released in late 1987.* ABOVE: No Rest for the Wicked *was Ozzy's fifth solo studio album.*

with my wife, take care of my kids, practice guitar, write songs, lift weights, and clean up Rottweiler dog shit. If anything gets beyond that, it gets confusing . . . that's why for Zakk Wylde's Black Label Society, the colors are black and white. There are no grey issues. Life is black and it's white. There's no in between. You're either an asshole or an all-right guy. I got no time for drama."

Recalling his audition for the band, he added, "Ozzy told me the day I met him and auditioned, 'Zakk, just be yourself and play with your heart and do what you do.' I'll take that beyond the grave. You can't fake being something you're not. Jimi Hendrix and Jimmy Page can't fake what they are, and the

Europe, plus Japan and Russia, where the band continued to be in demand.

Ozzy was also making waves in Russia with Zakk Wylde, Geezer Butler, and his new drummer, Randy Castillo. On August 12 and 13, his band played at the massive Moscow Music Peace Festival alongside Bon Jovi, Scorpions, Mötley Crüe, and many others. Not that everything was quite as successful in his home life. One night in his Buckinghamshire mansion, the singer worked his way through what has been reported to be as many as four bottles of vodka in a single marathon session, before

ABOVE: *Sabbath's fourteenth studio album,* Headless Cross, *restored some luster to the band's name.* **BELOW:** *A fan holding a SABBATH1 license plate at a show the Palladium club in New York in 1989.*

beautiful thing about those two guys is they are devoid of bullshit. Ozzy can't fake what he is. He's the real deal."

It must have been a slap in the face for Iommi when Ozzy recruited none other than Geezer Butler to play with him on the *No Rest for the Wicked* tour in 1989. In response, the guitarist asked the respected session bassist Neil Murray to accompany him on tour that summer. The new album, *Headless Cross*, released on April 29, 1989, contained some decent tunes once again, notably "When Death Calls," with its Wagnerian conclusion, and "Nightwing," later to inspire the name of a gothic metal band that adopted it in tribute. The album went some way toward alleviating the damage done to Sabbath's reputation by the feeble performance of *Eternal Idol*, reaching No. 32 in the UK, and the ensuing tour passed through America, the UK, and

Black Sabbath plays at the Mid-Hudson Civic Center in May 1989, featuring Tony Iommi (above), Tony Martin (top right), and Neil Murray (right).

walking up to his wife Sharon and saying, "I've decided you have to go." He then attempted to strangle her. The police arrived, arrested the singer, and threw him into the nearby police station at Amersham for the night. Impressively, his wife didn't press charges, although she did insist that he attend rehab afterward for a three-month stint.

By 1990, grunge was on its way down the line. Before that, Bill Ward emerged from semi-retirement to issue a solo album called *Ward One: Along the Way*. It was, he told me, "a big production for me, because I was wearing the artist's hat and the writer's hat as well as the producer's hat, and coordinating a lot of musicians. That's not an easy thing to do. Musicians have a whole lot of personality, as we all know, and I had to learn to be extremely patient. The biggest thing for me was being bold enough to get the very best out of them. Going to extremely experienced musicians and saying, 'I think there's another take in there,' was crossing a line for me! But we achieved a lot because they were all so flexible. The album made me stronger as a musician and a producer. It gave me great confidence, because I was finding my feet."

If only his old band would hurry up and do the same . . .

ABOVE: *In 1990, Ozzy released the live album,* Just Say Ozzy, *and Bill Ward emerged from semi-retirement to issue his debut solo album,* Ward One: Along the Way. **OPPOSITE:** *Ozzy and Zakk Wylde playing at Chicago's Poplar Creek Music Theater in July 1989.*

7

CALM BEFORE THE STORM

1991–1996

G runge, nu-metal, and alternative rock made life hard for Sabbath in the early-to-mid 1990s. It was a strange time for heavy metal in general: the well-funded industry was happy to tolerate most musicians' personal excesses in the 1980s, but a new, more serious, "authentic" dynamic emerged with the new music coming out of Seattle, making the old guard look, well, a touch silly.

That said, Black Sabbath had pulled itself out of the creative doldrums of the *Eternal Idol* era to some extent, with Tony Martin's expert vocals generally regarded by fans as a decent vehicle for Sabbath's songs. After the relative success of *Headless Cross*, the future looked brighter for Black Sabbath than it had in some time. Another album, *Tyr*, was set for release in the summer of 1990, and more than a few fans would be enthralled with "The Sabbath Stones," a seven-minute dinosaur of a song.

OPPOSITE: *The original Black Sabbath lineup of Ozzy Osbourne, Bill Ward, Tony Iommi, and Geezer Butler in a posed studio group shot in 1992.*

ABOVE: Tyr, *Black Sabbath's fifteenth studio album, was released in 1990.* **OPPOSITE:** *Sabbath members Tony Martin, Cozy Powell, and Tony Iommi photographed around 1990. Within a year, both Martin and Powell would be replaced by Ronnie James Dio and Vinny Appice, respectively.*

The *Tyr* tour was a success, with British and European dates lasting until November. Highlights included guest appearances at shows by Ian Gillan and Brian May, not to mention Geezer Butler, whose presence fueled rumors that a classic lineup reunion might be in the cards again. In fact, Butler took over the bass spot once more in December, displacing Murray.

Reunion fever was definitely in the air—and so the announcement came in January 1991 that Ronnie James Dio would be replacing Tony Martin. Drummer Vinny Appice took over from Cozy Powell, who had sustained an injury while riding a horse. As Appice told me, "I met Ronnie at some show

here and we talked, and then Cozy fell off the horse and broke his pelvis. Then I ran into them and they said, 'Why don't we get Vinny?' They called me, asked me if I wanted to do it, and I said yeah. Cozy was a big player in Sabbath, another ego in the band, and they were spending a lot of money and not getting very far with it. They were trying to work here in the US, but they didn't want to be here—they wanted to be in England. There were a lot of different things making it complicated with Cozy, so when I got in the band it was all smooth."

Dio knew what his role was as a member of Black Sabbath. As he told me, "The reason why my part of it was successful was because I brought musicality to that band. Before, what they did was great, but that band now had to move ahead, and what it did was, it moved itself into the '90s. It became very important in that genre because the music was approachable now. It wasn't something that had died ten years ago, which is what had happened before. Tony could not have been happier when I brought that musicality, and he was the person I was writing with, because Geezer left early on. He was there for about two days when I first joined the band, when they were living in Beverly Hills. Two days later, Geezer was gone: he wasn't in the band any more. He'd left. So the writing burden went to Tony and myself, which was fine for me—I'd rather work with a guitar player and not have too many minds involved in it, too many fingers in the pie, so we were able to cement this wonderful writing ability together."

He added, "It's so wonderful when you can do that—the singer and the guitarist aren't necessarily the most important members of a band, but they are the most visible, and so we became very good at that. I think I infused in Tony more of a place where he could go to be a better player, which he couldn't do before—play changes he couldn't do before, hear a melody that he didn't hear before that he would have to play to. So that was my part in it . . . I was enthusiastic, simply because I go into every project enthusiastically: if I don't, what the hell am I there for? I wanna be there going, 'This is great.' That's really what leaders do—I'm not saying I was the leader of that band, I'm not saying that at all—but if there was one, it was probably me at that time."

Dio paid his respects to Sabbath's former members too, explaining, "And if it wasn't me, it was Bill Ward. Which sounds strange, I know, but Billy took the bull by the horns and he wanted it to succeed. It was important that we all felt that way. Geezer didn't come back until we'd done a couple of tracks already. The way I saw it was, they had a chance to be as good as they really were, and I think on *Heaven and Hell* you really heard how good Tony and Geezer and Billy really were. You heard that, and that made me more proud than anything. That band got a chance to be successful again, and they deserved that success. That was a great time for me, knowing that I was there to help Black Sabbath be Black Sabbath again and it not be, 'Oh, they're a bunch of losers.'

"When we got together for *Mob Rules*, we had a process ready, so we could write songs," Dio recalled. "It doesn't mean that the songs were as good as they were on *Heaven and Hell*, but they were songs. It was more comfortable, but you know, that can sometimes be counter-productive as well. Sometimes you're really hungry when you do your best work. We'd had a big blockbuster success with *Heaven and Hell*, and the next album was slightly difficult to make because the success kinda got in the way."

When I asked Dio what had originally caused him to leave Sabbath around the *Live Evil* era, he told me, "Everybody was successful again, and it was like, 'Well, I gotta think about this . . . what, you're getting more than I am?' Wait a minute there, pal . . . all those things, those paranoia things that go on inside that band, came about, and it made it a lot more difficult. We had a drummer change, and the guys didn't like change a lot. Tony didn't mind so much, but Geezer really minded a lot. I think he always wanted it to be he, Ozzy, Tony, and Bill. And I understand that, that's fine; that's what got them there. But that wasn't reality; it wasn't going to happen. If Tony wasn't happy playing with Ozzy, then that was it, he was not gonna be there any more. At the end of the day, it's Tony who propelled that whole thing. My joy was really working with Tony from a writing perspective."

RETIRING AND DEHUMANIZING

Armed with its most accomplished singer, if not necessarily its most famous one, the latest version of Sabbath knuckled down to new music. Meanwhile, Ozzy had pulled through rehab and was making his best music in years in the form of 1991's *No More Tears*, recorded with longtime cohorts Zakk Wylde and Randy Castillo, and both Bob Daisley and new bassist Mike Inez. Motörhead's Ian "Lemmy" Kilmister assisted with the writing of the album's best song, "Mama, I'm Coming Home."

A No. 17 UK hit, *No More Tears* was a respectable success given how rapidly musical fashions were changing at this time, although Ozzy confounded expectations by announcing his intention to retire after the

album and tour cycle. It's been suggested since that he'd received a misdiagnosis of multiple sclerosis, but perhaps he simply missed his young family; or maybe he was just sick of the road. Either way, he announced a farewell show on November 15, 1992, in Costa Mesa, California.

At the same time, the Dio-fronted Sabbath

LEFT: *Ozzy released* No More Tears, *his sixth studio album, in September 1991.* **BELOW:** *Ozzy and longtime band member Zakk Wylde at a show at Brixton Academy on March 20, 1992. Just eight months later, Ozzy announced his retirement.*

ABOVE: *Ozzy's band, comprising Mike Inez, Zakk Wylde, Ozzy himself, and Randy Castillo, photographed in 1992.*
RIGHT: *A portrait of Ozzy taken around 1991.*

was making strides with a new album, *Dehumanizer*. Vinny Appice takes up the story. "I flew to England, we started writing and the same thing happened. I set up a little studio recording thing—in charge of the tapes again!—and by the time I got there they had three or four songs already written. We did the rest of the writing in about two weeks; everything was smooth again. We went in the studio and for the first six weeks Ronnie and

me had a house in Stafford: we rehearsed in the living room, with little amps—it was pretty funny! We demoed it at Monnow Valley, came back home for a couple of weeks, and then went back and recorded it at Rockfield. So it took two groups of six weeks to record."

When the album was released, on July 4, 1992, it made No. 33 on the UK chart—a respectable achievement given its juvenile cover art and the fact that the rock media clearly preferred alternative bands such as Nirvana and the Red Hot Chili Peppers. The song "TV Crimes" is a high point, with the technical riffing shared by Butler and Iommi a reminder of their advanced musicianship.

Butler, usually the quietest Sabbath member, was going through some struggles with the demon alcohol around this time. As he told me, "In 1992, we were in South America and I was trying to pick a fight with everybody. In the end, I nutted a statue. I completely split my eye open, and I was so drunk I didn't even know. I went to bed, and I woke up the next day and my head was stuck to the pillow. I couldn't figure out what was going on: I was covered in blood. Apparently I'd phoned my wife and gone nuts at her, having a big argument—but I couldn't remember anything about it.

"Then I got a phone bill for $2,000. It cost like eighty quid a minute, or something, to phone from South America. And I realized: what the hell am I doing to myself? So that was it, I didn't drink for two or three years. Then I started all over again, not being horrible but just doing it socially. I could have easily killed myself that night—I could have been shot or anything. I totally didn't remember any of it."

Vinny Appice is still proud of *Dehumanizer*. "I love that album," he told me. "It had a lot of fire in it. It has a lot of aggression and a great sound. Also, the drums are real loud on that album! Which is funny, because after we finished it we started mixing. It was pretty boring at Rockfield, so I said, 'You know, why don't I just fly home? You guys are pretty capable of mixing this.' And then, with me not being there, they were worried that the drums might not be loud enough! That's why

LEFT: *Now fronted by Dio once more, Sabbath released* **Dehumanizer**—*its sixteenth studio album—in 1992.* **OPPOSITE:** *The Sabbath lineup around the time of the* **Dehumanizer** *release.*

the drums are so loud: if I'd been there I would have suggested that they'd been a little lower. When Ronnie and I played it afterward, we were like, 'Holy shit, the drums are *loud*!'"

Dio reinforced this to me in a later interview, saying, "I think *Dehumanizer* is an highly underrated record. After we reformed I'm sure the media were thinking, now we're gonna get another *Heaven and Hell*. And the reaction was exactly the opposite, because that's not what we wanted to do. In going so dark, we alienated ourselves right away just

a little bit to the people who were expecting that. It was probably way, way too heavy for its time: the world was changing then, with boy bands and all that sort of stuff, and grunge. So it probably became a dinosaur right away, because it was out of its time.

"But most of the albums I've been involved with—and I hope it always goes this way—kind of become timeless, because of the songs' structure and the way they are, and because they're so unique and so different most of the time. You can listen to it twenty years later and think, wow, that's a good album—not wow, is that dated. Maybe in twenty years' time it will be dated, but maybe by then we'll be playing bricks, and that'll be the new sound. But I think most of my albums have stood the test of time, and that's probably the one thing I'm most proud of. You always get consistency with the things I've been involved with."

The tour rolled through South America in the month before the album's release, gained momentum as *Dehumanizer* took off, and passed through the States before arriving at Ozzy's final show at Costa Mesa. The original idea was that Dio, Iommi, Butler, and Ward would play first before Ozzy closed the show, but Dio himself was not keen on the idea.

Appice later told me that the inter-band relationships were becoming strained again, just as they had back in 1982. "The same thing started happening with them not getting along, and the thing that brought it to a head was the Ozzy show at Costa Mesa. They were offered by Sharon to play at Ozzy's retirement show: Black Sabbath would play and then Ozzy would go on. Tony and Geezer wanted to do it, but Ronnie didn't want to do it—he didn't want to open, so to speak, before Ozzy. He was also concerned that if he was on before Ozzy, that Sharon would turn his mic off or something . . . y'know, a technical difficulty! That kind of thing. So he didn't want to do it, and that was the end of the band. He said, 'I'm not doing it, and San Francisco is my last show.'"

PAGING ROB HALFORD

"We originally asked Tony Martin to replace him," Butler recalled, "but he couldn't get a visa on such short notice, so Rob Halford of Judas Priest offered to try. He's from Birmingham like us."

"Now I'm in the middle again," Appice continued, "so I talk to Tony and Geezer, I talk to Ronnie, I didn't want to leave them. If I left they'd be really screwed, because they have to get a singer and then a drummer in the two weeks before the show. I wanted to do it, so I explained to Ronnie that I couldn't leave them hanging—nothing against our relationship, unless you don't want me to do it—so I smoothed it out and they got Rob Halford to sing."

Halford, the most talented heavy metal singer that the UK has ever produced, was certainly an ideal candidate for his temporary job fronting Black Sabbath, as Appice recalled. "The next night we were in Arizona, and we had the next night off, so we rehearsed with Rob and went through the set list. It was cool but there wasn't much time for rehearsal. Poor Rob: 'Hey Rob, learn eleven songs and lyrics!' And then we changed the set because we didn't want to do so much Dio stuff. So now we're doing 'Symptom of the Universe' and all these other songs that I never really played—so now I gotta learn new songs too!"

On November 15, Sabbath delivered a solid set, although Halford experienced some difficulties. "We played the show and we pulled it off," Appice remembered. "Everybody said we sounded great, even

OPPOSITE AND ABOVE: *Ozzy Osbourne, Tony Iommi, and Geezer Butler put their handprints into the RockWalk of Fame.*

though Rob had a teleprompter to read the lyrics—and the thing broke! He's not twenty any more, so he can't see his lyric sheets—so he gets down on one knee to get closer to the sheets! He's doing that move onstage but really he's just trying to read the lyrics!"

Ozzy even joined his old band for four songs. Ward was ecstatic, telling me, "Ozzy just . . . came in! And I absolutely had a blast there. I couldn't find anything more pleasurable than to get up there with my friends and play. I absolutely had a blast . . . you know, we had a great time there. A wonderful time."

The set finished, Ozzy said his farewells to the crowd and walked offstage. Behind the scenes, however, plans for a full-scale Osbourne–Iommi–Butler–Ward reunion were being hatched, doctors having cleared Ozzy of any possible prognosis of multiple sclerosis.

Ward himself told me, "We worked for nine months on this project. After the Costa Mesa shows, we had our mind on this for at least for nine months. We had conversations with [Ozzy] by phone, and our managers were in touch. Many dates had already been scheduled before Ozzy decided not to carry on with the project."

Ozzy passed on the idea, but his retirement

CROSS PURPOSES

would turn out to be brief. For their part, Ronnie James Dio and Vinny Appice departed to re-form the band Dio, so Iommi called Tony Martin and asked if he would be interested in taking back his place in the band. The singer agreed, and a new drummer, Bobby Rondinelli, signed up too.

As the new sticks man told me, "I played with Doro Pesch for a while, and her tour manager Robert Gambino used to work for Sabbath. So I told Robert I really liked them, and it would be something I'd really like to do, and one day I get a call from Gambino telling me that Sabbath was looking for a drummer . . . I called [Iommi]. His wife answered the phone and I introduced myself. I said, 'I heard Sabbath is looking for a drummer and I'd love to check it out.' About ten minutes later, Iommi calls and says, 'Actually your name was on our list. I was gonna get in touch with you.' We talked for about an hour.

"We had a few more conversations and he said, 'Do you wanna join the band?' You know, with them you're either in the band or you're not! He said, 'Do you like to jam?' Because Tony likes to play off the cuff, and I love that stuff. I was weaned on that kind of music—Cream and freeform bands like that. We hit it off and that was it. The first time we jammed was in a house in Henley-in-Arden, near Birmingham. There was a house that the band rehearsed at, and I stayed there."

Once Martin, Iommi, Butler, Nicholls, and Rondinelli were installed in the Henley house, rehearsals for new material began. New songs were ready by summer 1993: Butler came up with the title for *Cross Purposes*, which was released on February 12, 1994. By then, the era of alternative rock and nu-metal had truly begun, making the industry environment even more difficult to navigate than before.

Of the album's best songs, "Virtual Death" was a throwback to the style of Sabbath's glory days, while "Immaculate Deception" featured an unusual, weighty guitar riff.

OPPOSITE AND RIGHT: Cross Purposes, *Sabbath's seventeenth studio album, was released in January 1994. A live version was recorded at the Hammersmith Apollo in London and released the following year.* **BELOW:** *Butler, Martin, Rondinelli, and Iommi at the Hammersmith Apollo in London on April 13, 1994, the show that became* Cross Purposes Live.

There were still plenty of ideas in Iommi's creative psyche, it appeared, and indeed *Cross Purposes* was a respectable album. The next step was a tour, and although the album only made No. 41 in the UK, ticket sales were strong. Support slots came from Motörhead and the death metal band Morbid Angel, then at their commercial peak.

In fact, Sabbath was starting to do well again, which made it all the more strange when Butler and Ward quit the band yet again. It seems Ward couldn't face Sabbath without Ozzy, and Butler had a falling out with Iommi over certain unrevealed issues—and he also wanted to start his own band, with a newer sound that would fit better with the modern metal of the day. Neil Murray and Cozy Powell came back to the fold in due course, but long-term fans began to wonder if the 1990s would only be about reunions and breakups for Sabbath.

FORBIDDEN

A CD/VHS (remember them?) live album titled *Cross Purposes Live* was the precursor in 1995 to yet another studio album, *Forbidden*, with which all of the Sabs' uncertainty about their role in modern music came to the fore. Looking for an updated sound, the band and its management recruited guitarist and producer Ernie C. from the band Body Count, who had produced demos for seminal acts such as Rage Against the Machine and Stone Temple Pilots, to produce the album.

Body Count had some edgy credibility, all right, thanks to a massive row in which they had been involved three years before. Led by rapper Ice-T, who wrote about murdering police officers in the 1992 song "Cop Killer," the group maintained a dangerous air that the members of Black Sabbath presumably wanted for themselves, hence Ernie C.'s role in the production chair. But the ruse smacked of desperation, especially as Body Count's songs were not especially well constructed or played during the band's early career.

Forbidden isn't bad. Like the rest of Sabbath's albums since *Heaven and Hell* fifteen years before, it contains some reasonably memorable songs while not threatening their revered early work in any way. The opening song, "Illusion of Power" has its moments—some spooky vocals and laughter, plus Ice-T's guest vocals, which take the form of a semi-spoken rant. "You're caught in a complex catacomb of your own inadequacies and pitiful weaknesses!" he intones with a certain eloquence, before fading out amid screams and feedback.

Of the song, Ice-T informed me, "Sabbath admired Body Count—they could listen to our songs like 'There Goes the Neighborhood' and hear Sabbath in it—so they reached out to Ernie and they produced 'Illusion of Power.'" Working with Iommi et al had left its mark on the rapper: "When they come walking through the door, you're like, 'Holy shit, I've been really fortunate to have worked with some very cool people!'"

Sabbath then took off on tour for most of the rest of the year. In June 1995 the band played in Denmark and Sweden before heading to North America once again, traveling through the States and Canada before winding up in California. A lengthy tour through Germany, Poland, Hungary, Italy,

OPPOSITE: *Sabbath's eighteenth studio album,* Forbidden, *was released in 1995.* ABOVE: *Rapper Ice-T provided guest vocals to the opening song of* Forbidden, *"Illusion of Power."*

Switzerland, Austria, Scandinavia, the UK, and the Far East brought the band through to the autumn, coinciding with the release of Geezer Butler's debut solo album, *Plastic Planet*, which he recorded with a band he named G/Z/R.

"I've always done my own stuff," Butler explained. "On most of the [Sabbath] songs I got the bass line straight away, especially on the first three albums where I just followed the guitar riff. We didn't have time to think about it anyway, because we only had a couple of days

ABOVE: *Sabbath playing at New York's Roseland Ballroom on the* Forbidden *tour in July, 1995.* **RIGHT:** *Geezer Butler chose 1995 to release his debut solo album,* Plastic Planet. **OPPOSITE:** *Geezer Butler photographed in 1995 after the release of* Plastic Planet.

to record the whole album. We'd play them live and then alter them slightly as we went along."

Meanwhile, Ozzy was in the best shape of his life, having become sober and physically fit. He issued a US-only album called *Live and Loud* in the summer of '95 to keep fans happy while he worked on his new release, *Ozzmosis.* The latter was released on November 4, and was another reasonably well-crafted set of songs based around Zakk Wylde's astonishing guitar playing.

So far, the 1990s had treated Ozzy fairly well and Sabbath with a kind of ambivalence, given that popular guitar music was so different from the sounds either act was making. Something was about to change, though, and that change effectively came about thanks to the efforts of one person: Sharon Osbourne.

BELOW: *In the best shape of his life, Ozzy released his seventh solo album,* Ozzmosis, *in November 1995.*
RIGHT: *Ozzy, photographed in a New York recording studio in May 1995 working on* Ozzmosis.

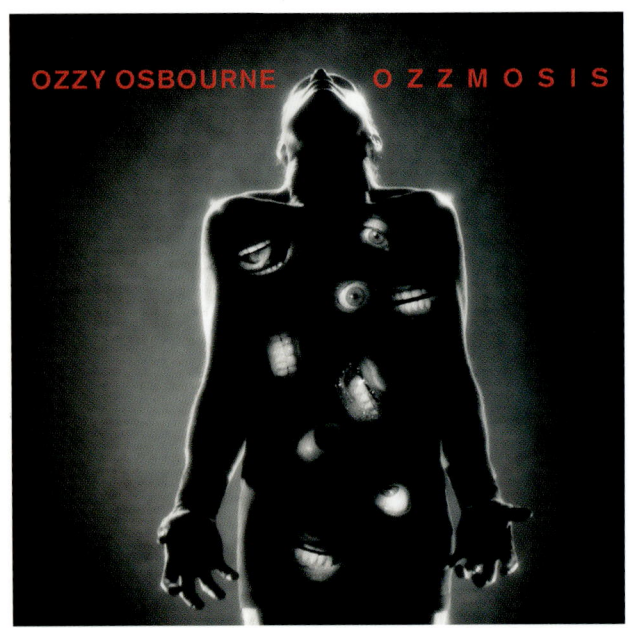

"Meanwhile, Ozzy was in the best shape of his life, having become sober . . ."

MAD SABBATH

OZZY OSBOURNE

Urinating on the Alamo Cenotaph

It is well documented that Ozzy Osbourne—possibly fueled by a couple of medicinal sherries—went out in search of booze on February 19, 1982 in San Antonio, Texas. Dressed in his wife Sharon's dress because she had hidden his clothes in a futile attempt to stop him finding a bar, he stopped for a quick moment of urinary relief against what he assumed was some old stone wall. To his chagrin, the local cops didn't see the funny side of him urinating on the Alamo Cenotaph and banned him from playing in San Antonio again.

Missing 24 Hours of His Life

In the early hours one morning in 1978, Ozzy walked drunkenly into the wrong room of Sabbath's Nashville hotel, assuming it was his assigned room. The maid fled in terror and the inebriated singer passed out on the bed. Show time came later that day and, of course, Ozzy couldn't be found; the gig was duly cancelled. The next day he appeared, querulously asking when the show was taking place.

Biting the Head Off a Bat

It was in Des Moines, Iowa, on January 20, 1982, that Ozzy saw what he assumed was a rubber bat near him on stage. In fact it was a real, living bat, thrown at him by some callous audience member. Imagine Ozzy's surprise when he bit its head off for a laugh and then had to endure rabies shots after the show . . . and thirty years of journalists asking him about it. In 1981 he did the same thing to two doves in a meeting at CBS. Why? Only he knows.

GEEZER BUTLER

Climbing Up Walls

Bill Ward once recalled that Sabbath's bassist came running into a dressing room and attempted to climb the wall. The drummer later asserted that speed was involved. You don't say?

Headbutting a Statue

In 1992, Geezer decided to vent his anger by headbutting a statue. His face didn't thank him for it. Booze may have been involved.

RONNIE JAMES DIO

Losing a Thumb in a Garden Gnome Incident

One of the late, great Dio's thumbs was once severed by a falling garden gnome while he was engaged in some yard work. "It was a killer garden gnome," he joked at the time. "The first thought that flashed into my mind was, 'How on earth am I going to make my devil-horns sign now?" Fortunately, the hapless digit was surgically reattached.

BILL WARD

Voluntarily Being Set on Fire

Bill Ward, a splendid fellow in many ways, was often the victim of intra-band pranks in Sabbath's early days. Iommi was particularly fond of setting him on fire with the aid of various inflammable agents. Once, as the guitarist recalled, Ward actually urged Iommi to do so, but soon regretted it when the latter overdid the gasoline and he came close to suffering very serious burns.

GLENN HUGHES

Getting Beaten Up by a Mad Tour Manager

During Glenn Hughes's tenure as Black Sabbath's singer, the band's tour manager was a chap named John Downing, who later died in mysterious circumstances (he is thought to have jumped or been thrown from a cross-Channel ferry). In life, he was cursed with a short temper, and once punched Hughes so hard that he broke his eye socket and caused the singer to lose his voice, thanks to the blood which poured from his nose into his throat. Hughes recalled, "I woke up the next day with the biggest black eye you've ever seen. He'd hit me on the nose and my left eye socket, which shattered. Some bone from that socket went down into the back of my nose, and perforated something. Without me knowing, blood was being stored on my vocal cords in my throat."

Getting Tied to a Chair by a Mad Girlfriend

As Hughes recalled in his 2011 autobiography, "One night, my girlfriend and I got into an altercation over this really amazing gold chain that she had. I grabbed her chain in my hand and twisted it, and she freaked. It was reparable, but she hit out at me, deservedly so. Her mother heard this altercation and came into the room with her gun. My girlfriend was pretty pissed at me and sided with her mother—even though she usually sided with me against her parents. So they proceeded to tie me to a chair with rope!" Fortunately the two females were moved to pity and let the singer go after some stern words.

TONY IOMMI

Astral Projection

As Iommi recounted in his excellent 2011 autobiography, as a younger man he mastered the art of "leaving" his body during meditation. Apparently it was a pleasant experience, although it's not immediately clear how useful the skill would be.

IAN GILLAN

Joining Black Sabbath While Drunk

Who goes to the pub with Tony Iommi and Geezer Butler, gets splendidly drunk and wakes up the next day having no memory of joining their band? Clue: his first name is Ian, and he used to sing in Deep Purple. The title "Black Purple" was inevitably given to Sabbath's new line-up—not a bad name, as it happens.

Crashing Cars While Drunk

In the song "Trashed," Gillan sings merrily about taking Bill Ward's new car for a spin after a glass or two of liquor. The inevitable occurred and Gillan smashed the vehicle to pieces. One can only assume that the two patched it up over a small snifter of something soothing.

8

THE RETURN

1996-2005

By 1996, "alternative" was the buzzword in rock music, so much so that more or less anything went in terms of the music and image of a whole new wave of bands as long as nothing reminded people of the old music from the '80s and, heaven forbid it, the '70s. Nu-metal was in full swing, with Korn, Coal Chamber, Rage Against the Machine, Linkin Park, and Limp Bizkit all in business or on their way; grunge had survived the death of Nirvana's Kurt Cobain in 1994, against all expectations, with Pearl Jam, Soundgarden, Alice in Chains, and Stone Temple Pilots all doing very nicely, thank you; and a wave of maverick artists like Tool and Marilyn Manson were redefining experimental music that the masses liked.

Little wonder, then, that Lollapalooza, the achingly cool traveling festival founded by Perry Farrell of Jane's Addiction and Porno for Pyros, didn't want Ozzy on the bill when his wife Sharon Osbourne put in a request for a slot. Fuming from the insult, she founded a new festival, Ozzfest, which overlapped slightly with the Lollapalooza ethos

OPPOSITE: *Black Sabbath, consisting of the original foursome, playing at the UK Music Hall of Fame in 2005.*

ABOVE: *Geezer's second non-Sabbath album,* **Black Science,** *was released in 1997.* **OPPOSITE:** *Group portrait of Black Sabbath showing Geezer Butler, Ozzy Osbourne, and Tony Iommi, in Amsterdam in 1998.*

(Metallica played both festivals, for example) but which focused much more on metal, and indeed nu-metal, making it instantly the most desirable bill in America for hundreds of wannabe stars.

Meanwhile, post-*Forbidden*, Black Sabbath seemed to have run out of gas. Iommi spent time working on material for a solo album, due to feature several guest vocalists, including Rob Halford and Glenn Hughes, but decided not to release it, although a tape leaked and was inevitably made available shortly afterward on the internet, or at least the fledgling file-sharing networks that were slowly growing in prominence. Iommi must have taken a keen interest in the inaugural Ozzfest of summer and autumn 1996, which

featured Slayer, Danzig, Biohazard, Sepultura, and Fear Factory on the main stage and a second stage featuring Earth Crisis, Powerman 5000, Neurosis, Coal Chamber, and Cellophane.

In 1997, Sharon contacted Iommi and asked him if he was interested in reforming the classic 1970s Black Sabbath lineup for Ozzfest's second year, and he agreed. Geezer Butler was quick to sign up, too, telling me, "I always remember, I'd just done my first solo project, *Plastic Planet*, and I was doing press for that and they asked me if Sabbath would ever get back together. And I said, no way! Never in a month of Sundays. And then the very next week, Ozzy phoned up and said, 'Do you want to do Ozzfest this year as Sabbath?' And we were like, yeah!"

"Sharon called and asked me if I wanted to do it," Butler said. "She wanted to have us as the headliners with Ozzy at this year's Ozzfest because of the festival's success last year. I said yes, then it had to be put together quickly because there were only two months to rehearse."

Sharon and Ozzy invited Black Sabbath to close the show for Ozzfest '97, after Ozzy had performed his own songs with his band. However, Bill Ward was not asked to play; his place on the Ozzfest was taken by Mike Bordin, the drummer in Faith No More and Ozzy's own band.

"I got passed over, and I didn't like that," Ward told me. "It was a very, *very* bitter pill. I felt totally betrayed. I've never completely known the reason for being passed over,

but I have a feeling that there might have been some Sharon influence going on there. Maybe I was regarded as a loose cannon, or that I wasn't really up for it, but I have the feeling that maybe some decisions were made without me being consulted in the first place. I was ready to fuckin' go out there and kick ass . . . you can't just show up and play. It takes me a while to get everything back into the groove and get everything working."

On May 24, 1997, the Ozzfest headlined by Black Sabbath began in Bristow, Virginia, and featured on its main stage, in reverse order, Powerman 5000, Machine Head, Fear Factory, Type O Negative, and Pantera, before

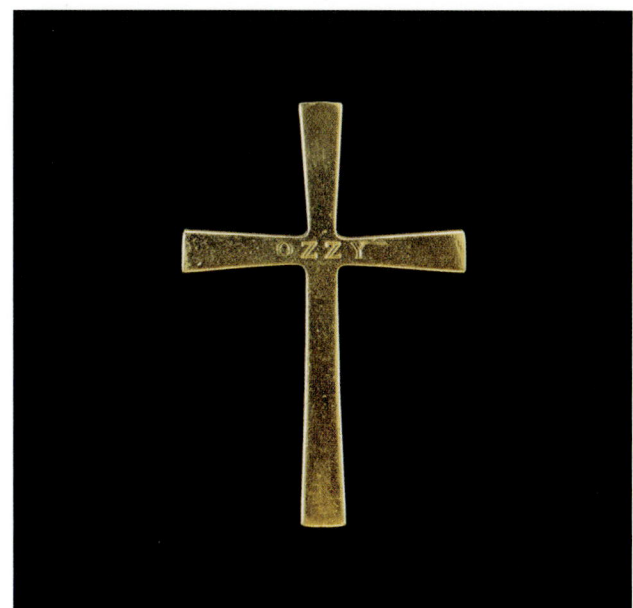

OPPOSITE TOP: *Bill Ward and his new band in 1997, around the time of the release of* When the Bough Breaks.
OPPOSITE BOTTOM: When the Bough Breaks, *Bill Ward's second solo album, was released in April 1997.* LEFT: The Ozzman Cometh *was a solo compilation album released by Ozzy in 1997.*
BELOW: *Ozzy performing with Black Sabbath at Ozzfest in 1997.*

the two-band Ozzy extravaganza. The second stage featured Vision of Disorder, Drain STH, Coal Chamber, Slo-Burn, and Neurosis before headliners Downset, attracting hardcore punks, stoner rockers, goths, and straight-ahead metal fans in droves.

The festival played in Florida, North Carolina, Texas, Illinois, Pennsylvania, New Jersey, Missouri, Michigan, Minnesota, Wisconsin, Colorado, Nevada, and Arizona before ending on June 29 in San Bernardino, California. On June 17, at the Polaris Amphitheater in Columbus, Ohio, the Ozzy/ Sabbath section of the gig was canceled when Ozzy's throat gave out. The fans at the venue were consoled by a quickly assembled supergroup made up of members of Pantera, Type O Negative, Fear Factory, and others, who played "I Don't Know," "Mr. Crowley," "Suicide Solution," "Crazy Train," and "Bark at the Moon." The Ozzfest returned on July 1 for a make-up show. Bordin was unavailable for that date, so Ozzy and Sabbath used drummer Shannon Larkin of Ugly Kid Joe and Godsmack for the occasion.

BILL WARD RETURNS

In late 1997, a Black Sabbath live album was scheduled to be recorded, and this time Ward was asked to participate. As he told me, the Sabbath fan base had been unhappy that Bordin had taken his place in the Ozzfest lineup. "A lot of them were pissed. Those that knew the original band were like, what the fuck is going on, you know? It was a real uncomfortable thing to go through. I just watched it happen. I mean, I know Mike Bordin, he's a buddy of mine, and he's often referred to me and my chops in certain songs, and he asks, how does this work in certain songs?

"Eventually all that got worked out. After they finished doing the first Ozzfest with Mike, Tony was the first to call me. I felt really lucky that I was allowed to take part in the reunion, when it finally happened . . . Ozzy coming back in 1997 opened the door for me. It released me from my own self-made exile, you know, because that was what it felt like. It was so hard not to pick up the phone. One of the things that encouraged me to try and work out things for myself was knowing that I couldn't just sit around on my ass . . . it was sweet and sour. I'd started to move ahead and try to create some of my own things, but I missed them all the time. I missed them spiritually and I missed them physically, all the fuckin' time. Especially when I'd hear their new music, and I'd hear Tony's stuff, and I'd see Geezer hanging out with Ozz and whatever."

RIGHT: *Bill Ward returns to Black Sabbath to man the drum kit, photographed here in December 1997.*

The official reunion shows took place on December 4 and 5, 1997, with Fear Factory in support. The venue was the NEC Arena in Birmingham, England, Sabbath's home town; the shows were recorded on a mobile studio facility and produced by Bob Marlette at Rockfield Studios and elsewhere. Two new songs, "Psycho-Man" and "Selling My Soul," were duly laid down for the live album, which was called *Reunion*.

On December 22, Ozzy was a special guest on the American TV show *Late Night with Conan O'Brien*. Audiences must have found it strange for O'Brien to be interviewing this eccentric character, but in retrospect it's evident that someone at MTV must have been watching—based on the events to come.

A full Black Sabbath tour was booked for June 1998, and the *Reunion* live album was scheduled for release in October. In due course, Sabbath began rehearsals for the summer tour in the old house in Monmouth that the band had been using since the early days, although those plans were temporarily derailed when Ward suffered a heart attack on May 19. The episode was serious enough for him to require angioplasty on June 3, but a full recovery was predicted—as long as he maintained a healthy lifestyle.

On June 20, 1998, Ozzy and Black Sabbath appeared consecutively once again atop a UK Ozzfest bill comprising Foo Fighters, Therapy?, Pantera, Slayer, Soulfly, and Fear Factory. The second stage featured Coal Chamber plus

OPPOSITE: *Ozzy Osbourne and Tony Iommi photographed at a reunion show in Birmingham in December 1997.* **BELOW:** *Black Sabbath at an October 1998 store appearance in Tower Records in New York's Times Square.*

Life of Agony, Limp Bizkit, Neurosis, Human Waste Project, Entombed, and Pitchshifter. The venue, the Milton Keynes Bowl in Buckinghamshire, had hosted a landmark heavy metal gig featuring Metallica and Megadeth five years previously.

The *Reunion* album appeared in October and made the headlines thanks to a record-signing "tour" that the band carried out in eight US cities. Ward had recovered well from his heart surgery, but as a backup in case of any problems, Vinny Appice was asked to accompany Sabbath for the tour. As he recalled, "Sharon said, 'I want you there just in case something happens: Bill's had a mild heart attack, no one knows what could happen with the guy.' So for the first ten days or two weeks of the tour, I was on the side of the stage, hands taped up, dressed, ready to jump on if he fell over or something crazy like that happened. Funnily enough, because I was on the side of the stage, Ozzy would always try to dump a bucket of water on me. He never got me, though—I always got out of the way in time!"

As time passed, Appice's presence was less essential. "It became obvious that Bill wasn't having any problems, so I started walking into the audience a little to check out the show. Actually, I started taking digital pictures for Sony, and posting them on my website so that fans could check out the shows from the night before, because I was able to go anywhere— the dressing rooms, places you'd never see. So then I started taking pictures from the audience: after three weeks I was out by the soundboard and thinking, if anything happens

OPPOSITE: *Ozzy with Black Sabbath at Houston's Bank One Ballpark on New Year's Eve in 1998.* ABOVE: Reunion *is a live album released by Black Sabbath in 1998. It was the first recording of the four original members since Ozzy was fired in 1979.*

to Bill I'll just run! But as time went on I just became more loose with where I was going. In fact, everybody else got sick—Tony got a bad flu, Ozzy had a cold, but Bill was rocking."

The *Reunion* tour—which featured support from Pantera once again, plus other bands such as Incubus, Deftones, and System of a Down— continued into the spring of 1999, but it seemed the good times were set to be brief. The announcement came in April 1999 that Sabbath would headline the forthcoming Ozzfest, with Ozzy performing double duties, as he had done two years previously; more dates were set for December, building up to a final show at the Birmingham NEC, which would be billed as "The Last Supper"—Sabbath's last ever gig.

Sabbath owned Ozzfest '99. With the main stage featuring Rob Zombie, Deftones, Slayer, Primus, Godsmack, and System of a Down, and the second stage featuring Fear Factory, Static-X, Slipknot, Puya, Drain STH, Hed(pe), Apartment 26, Flashpoint, and Pushmonkey, the event kicked off at Florida's West Palm Beach and worked its way down through Georgia, Tennessee, North Carolina, Virginia, and New Jersey, winding up after two long sweeps across the States in New York in August.

After four months off, Sabbath began the *Last Supper* tour. After playing London followed by dates in the Netherlands, Finland, Sweden, and Germany, the final stage was set for December 21 and 22 in Birmingham. Sabbath was still adamant that these shows would be its last. The shows were filmed for a DVD and VHS entitled *The Last Supper*, released in June 2000.

Could this really be the end for Black Sabbath? Well, we're not quite at the end of the book yet . . .

OPPOSITE: *Sabbath playing at Bank One Ballpark in Houston on New Years' Eve 1998 on the* Reunion *tour.*
THIS PAGE: *Ozzy (above left), Iommi (above), and Butler (left) playing at Ozzfest in New Jersey in June 1999.*

"SHARRRONNNNNNN!"

In 1999, Ozzy was busier than ever, having resumed his solo career. By now he had six children but, aged only fifty-one, he apparently had plenty of fuel left in the tank, albeit in industry mode rather than as a creative musician. He and Sharon busied themselves around this time with a record company, Divine Recordings, distributed by Priority and designed to handle Ozzfest-related releases, plus those by a handful of other bands, such as Slaves on Dope. Another significant album release by Divine was Tony Iommi's solo record, *Iommi*, which appeared on October 30, 2000.

ABOVE: Iommi, *the debut solo album by Tony Iommi, was released in 2000 after nearly five years of planning.*
BELOW: *A posed portrait of Ozzy Osbourne in a dressing room, sitting on a director's chair.* **OPPOSITE:** *A promotional photo for* The Osbournes, *an MTV show that followed Ozzy, Sharon, and two of their children.*

By 2001, the Ozzfest was the premier tour for rock and metal in America. As the festival grew to dominate the market, so the public profiles of Ozzy and Sharon began to outgrow the confines of the music scene. The latter was asked for management advice from artists such as Limp Bizkit's Fred Durst, Guns N' Roses, and Courtney Love.

To no one's great surprise, Black Sabbath reformed for the 2001 Ozzfest, although cynicism was mostly restrained among the fan base simply because of the huge presence of the festival, and also because of the arrival later the same year of a new MTV show, *The Osbournes*, which purported to follow the singer and Sharon, plus two of their children, Kelly and Jack, and their many dogs, in a reality-TV format. Ozzy's new album, *Down to Earth*, also appeared that year amid a swirl of

LEFT: *Sabbath on stage with a burning cross in 2001.*
ABOVE: **Down to Earth** *is Ozzy's eighth studio album, released on October 2001.*

Osbourne activity that saw the man's profile rise to stratospheric levels.

Asked by this author a decade later if he recalled the show fondly, Ozzy ruminated, "You go to bed one day and you wake up the next day and the world's completely different. Everywhere there's fucking cameras, you get attacked by the fucking things. The kids couldn't handle it; my wife couldn't handle it . . . on the one hand it was phenomenal, on the other hand I had to watch my family suffer. But we invented a new form of television. We started the ball rolling for all these fuckin' new shows now. Would we do it again? I dunno. I don't think so."

Sabbath, Ozzy, and the Ozzfest were now a three-headed industry institution that generated tens—perhaps hundreds—of millions of dollars in revenue per year. Sabbath's

ABOVE: *Ozzy and members of his family at the 2000 Grammy Awards in Los Angeles.* **OPPOSITE:** *Ozzy and Sharon in May 2002 at the White House Correspondents' Dinner; President Bush even mentioned Ozzy in his speech.*

classic albums were compiled, reissued, and re-reissued throughout the decade in a variety of audio and visual formats. As Butler told me, "The catalogue's still selling millions. The reissues are just the way the record companies work these days—old stuff seems to be outselling the new stuff for some reason."

Ozzy embarked on a US tour in 2002, supporting the *Down to Earth* album and taking Rob Zombie with him in support, but ten dates from it were rescheduled after he suffered a stress fracture to his leg after falling in the shower before a show in Tucson, Arizona. This was the first of a series of

setbacks he suffered in this period, although the early years of the millennium were also filled with commercial success thanks to *The Osbournes*. By 2002 he was a visible presence on chat shows, in movie cameos, and as a special guest to the great and the good of the industry and even politics. This would have been unimaginable before the Ozzfest launched just six years before.

The Osbournes was genuinely entertaining. With its Rat Pack–style lounge theme version of Ozzy's 1980 hit "Crazy Train," the series was filmed by twelve cameras installed in the Osbournes' house—a palatial L.A. residence with a sculpted pool, dozens of rooms, and a roving camera crew. There was a certain air of voyeurism about it, for sure, which some viewers didn't appreciate. None other than sometime Sex Pistol John Lydon told me, "Ozzy's hilarious, but I felt sorry for him when his wife orchestrated that terrible, *terrible* MTV production, because I thought it was humiliating for him. It was like a Victorian mental asylum where you pay a penny to prod the loony with a stick."

Within a few episodes of its launch, the show was attracting six million viewers a week in America—making it MTV's most-watched show ever at the time—and it scored a proportionally similar audience in the UK when it debuted on Channel 4 in March 2002. All of this helped to make Ozzy's February–May 2002 world tour a success: he was even asked to play for US servicemen stationed in Japan and Korea. While he was in Japan, a Tokyo show was filmed for later release on a DVD titled *Live at Budokan*.

On May 6, Ozzy and Sharon appeared at the 88th Annual White House Correspondents' Association Dinner at the Hilton in Washington,

D.C., hosted by President George W. Bush. Bush even mentioned Ozzy in his speech, saying, "The thing about Ozzy is, he's made a lot of big hit recordings—'Party with Animals,' 'Sabbath Bloody Sabbath,' 'Facing Hell,' 'Black Skies,' and 'Bloodbath In Paradise.' Ozzy . . . Mom loves your stuff." The world cringed.

GOING THROUGH CHANGES

The drama continued in an incredibly eventful couple of years. In 2002, Sharon defeated colon cancer; Kelly launched a music career, signing to Epic alongside Ozzy and releasing an album called *Shut Up* that contained a cover version of Madonna's "Papa Don't Preach"; Ozzy's bassist, Robert Trujillo, joined Metallica, his place taken by former Metallica bassist Jason Newsted (who quit for still-unexplained reasons shortly afterward); Jack Osbourne entered rehab for an addiction to Oxycontin; Ozzy and Kelly switched labels to Sanctuary and recorded a version of Black Sabbath's "Changes" as a duet; Sharon was given her own syndicated TV show, *The Sharon Osbourne Show*, and joined *The X Factor* as a judge; and Ozzy suffered a quad-bike accident that left him close to death in December 2003.

Eight broken ribs, a punctured lung, a smashed collarbone, severe concussion, and a crushed neck vertebra were the net result of the crash, which also left Ozzy with no memory of eleven days of his life. Eight of those days were spent in a coma after the accident, which took place at the Osbournes' country estate in Buckinghamshire, fortunately not far from a major hospital, Slough's Wexham Park facility. Somehow he was up and running again in time for Ozzfest 2004, which was to be headlined once again by Black Sabbath. The same year, Iommi released a second solo album, this time with singer Glenn Hughes, titled *The 1996 Dep Sessions*: the legitimate version of an album

OPPOSITE: *Kelly Osbourne performing "Papa Don't Preach" at the 2002 MTV Movie Awards.* LEFT: *Iommi and Glenn Hughes in 2005, around the release of their album* Fused. TOP AND ABOVE: *Iommi's second and third solo albums,* The 1996 Dep Sessions, *released in 2004, and* Fused, *released in 2005, were both collaborative works with Glenn Hughes.*

The tour rolled through America, starting in Boston and featuring Shadows Fall, In Flames, Killswitch Engage, Mastodon, the Haunted, Arch Enemy, and Soilwork. On certain dates it was noted that Iron Maiden singer Bruce Dickinson appeared to be a little discontented, dropping some veiled comments from the stage. This came to a head during Maiden's final scheduled date with the Ozzfest on August 20, in Devore, California.

During the set, Maiden was pelted with eggs and other items from the front of the stage, and the power was cut on some occasions, interrupting the band's set. It was also reported that a chant of "Ozzy, Ozzy" had been heard through the P.A. system during Maiden's performance. After the set, Sharon Osbourne took the stage, and in a statement to the crowd called Dickinson a "prick."

Sharon later released a further statement admitting that she had been behind the power cuts, although she did not claim responsibility

he and Hughes had recorded back in 1996, which had since been bootlegged.

By now, the classic-rock music format had been widely accepted by the industry and the public, and both Sabbath and the group's individual members were largely welcomed wherever they went. Fans asked for a new studio album, having been denied one since *Forbidden*, but none was immediately forthcoming—although the band was rarely out of the public eye. A spat with Iron Maiden was notable in 2005 because Sabbath didn't come out of it looking good.

This took place during Ozzfest 2005, the bill for which was one of the most prestigious yet. Fans of classic British metal were treated to the spectacular sight of Iron Maiden playing before the headliners, Black Sabbath. These two great bands on a single bill made for a dream combination for many attendees.

OPPOSITE TOP: *In 2004, Sabbath released a collection of their first eight albums in a compilation named* Black Box.
OPPOSITE BELOW: *Geezer Butler's third solo album,* Ohmwork, *was released in 2005.* **ABOVE:** *Iron Maiden performing at Ozzfest 2005 at the PNC Bank Arts Center in New Jersey.*

ABOVE: *Tony Iommi with Clive Burr and Iron Maiden in November 2005 at the Hard Rock Café in London.* OPPOSITE: *Under Cover is Ozzy's ninth solo studio album.*

for the egg throwing. "For twenty shows we were forced to hear Dickinson's nightly outbursts from the stage: 'When we come back to America, we'll be back with a proper sound system,' or 'We won't be playing the same old songs every night [like Sabbath],' 'We don't need a teleprompter [like Ozzy]' and 'We don't need a reality show to be legit [again, like Ozzy].' Was Dickinson so naive as to think that I was going to let him get away with talking shit about my family night after night? I don't think he realizes who he's dealing with." She signed off as "the real Iron Maiden."

The incident made a serious impact. Maiden's manager Rod Smallwood claimed that he had "never seen anything anywhere near as disgusting and unprofessional as what went on that night," and press officers for the two camps seemed to be feeding e-mailed updates to the press on an almost daily basis at one point.

I asked Ozzy what had happened, and he told me, "You know what? Unbeknown to me, every night [Dickinson] was going onstage slagging me off. And that wasn't fair. If he didn't like the fuckin' tour, he should have said, 'I'm jumping [off] the fuckin' tour,' but to go onstage and fuckin' slag me off for no reason . . . I'd never said a fuckin' bad thing to him.

"The bass player [Steve Harris] came 'round at the last gig and said, 'I'm sorry about Bruce,' and I'm like, 'What the fuck are you talking about?' Nobody had told me, you know. I said, 'You know what? I don't understand what the fuck you're talking about here.' And so, I mean,

Sharon got pissed off . . . it was nothing to do with me. I suppose Sharon got pissed off. I'll back my wife up to the hilt, but I didn't know what was going down."

What annoyed Ozzy most about the whole situation was the childishness of it. "If you've got something to talk to me about, be a man. Come to my face and say, 'I think you're a fuckin' asshole.' . . . But to go on my stage and start slagging me off—that ain't fair." Dickinson and his bandmates, he noted, were making "a few fuckin' quid out of that Ozzfest. They weren't fucking slagging me off when they got paid every fucking night."

And that, apart from a covers album from Ozzy called *Under Cover*, was it for this frenetic period of his career. Would it get any easier in 2006 and beyond? What do you think?

LUCKY NUMBERS

2006–2016

Ozzy Osbourne's solo career was his first priority in 2006, and why not? He had outstripped Black Sabbath in terms of sheer sales and media presence some years previously, although, when *The Osbournes* ran its course after its fourth season in 2005, the public hysteria surrounding him diminished slightly. He remained in the limelight, of course, not least when he agreed to appear in a TV advertising spot for a product called I Can't Believe It's Not Butter. The brand's owner, Unilever, spent £7 million on the ad, which featured Ozzy and TV impressionist Jon Culshaw shambling around in a kitchen.

OPPOSITE: *Sabbath on stage at New York's Madison Square Garden during* The End *tour on February 25, 2016. The tour has been billed as the band's farewell.* **ABOVE:** Black Rain, *released in 2007, is Ozzy's tenth solo album.*

As neither Tony Iommi nor Geezer Butler had particularly stellar solo careers to fall back on, it made total sense for them to form a new group, once more with old allies, but under a new name. Heaven and Hell was the new outfit's title, and it featured Ronnie James Dio and Vinny Appice in their third partnership with the Sabbath musicians. The timing could not have been better, with Sabbath being entered into the Rock and Roll Hall of Fame the same year and Dio now one of the classic-rock world's most loved singers.

TOP: *In 2006, Heaven and Hell—composed of Iommi and Butler along with Ronnie James Dio and Vinny Appice—played to a packed audience at New York's Radio City Music Hall.* **ABOVE:** *The 2007 release from Heaven and Hell,* Live from Radio City Music Hall. **OPPOSITE:** *The four members of Heaven and Hell in a staged studio shot in 2007.*

Bill Ward didn't take part in Heaven and Hell. Why? Only he knows. Perhaps his health and sobriety were taking up the majority of his attention. As he told me in 2005, "I had a heart problem seven years ago, so I try to look after myself. I walk a lot and I do a lot of rigorous exercise, and I try to keep myself really active.

"I'll leave counseling to the counselors," he added, "those who know something! In my private life I spend a lot of time with other alcoholics. I talk about it all the time. I help them, and by helping them I help myself. If they want to get sober, I help them. I've been on the 12-Step program for a long time. I went through nine hospitals, all told, which is not unusual. But I got cleaned up Stateside, eventually. I'm in my twenty-second year of sobriety now."

I asked him if he'd gone through counseling in the wake of sobering up. "Yes—after I got sober I realized there were a lot of things going on with me that I didn't know about," he told me. "I went to therapy for certain things, but I don't do my recovery every day because I'm craving for a drink, it's nothing to do with that. I do my recovery every day in order to have a really decent life, and what I mean by a decent life is the way that I feel on the inside. I don't mean, I'm going to be a fuckin' millionaire or anything like that: in fact, it's quite the opposite of material possessions, you know. It's about your own strength . . . it's made it easier to be everything. I've been really discovering myself as a musician in the last twenty-two years. I didn't even know who the hell I was until I started getting sober. I'm

still discovering all kinds of things about me, and I push myself as far as I can push myself. As a drummer, I've got so much to learn. And I push myself as a musician and a dad. I feel like I'm at the beginning of my life, most days."

WIND AND RAIN

Interest in Heaven and Hell was piqued still further by the release of *Black Sabbath: The Dio Years*, a compilation of songs gathered from the four Black Sabbath albums featuring Ronnie James Dio. To add incentive to buy the album, the label responsible for it, Rhino, asked Iommi and Dio if they would record a couple of new songs for it, and they said yes.

In the thirteen years since the two men had worked together, times had changed: grunge and nu-metal had been and gone, and a whole new classic rock scene had come to the fore, as chronicled by the British magazine of the same name. None of that mattered when the new

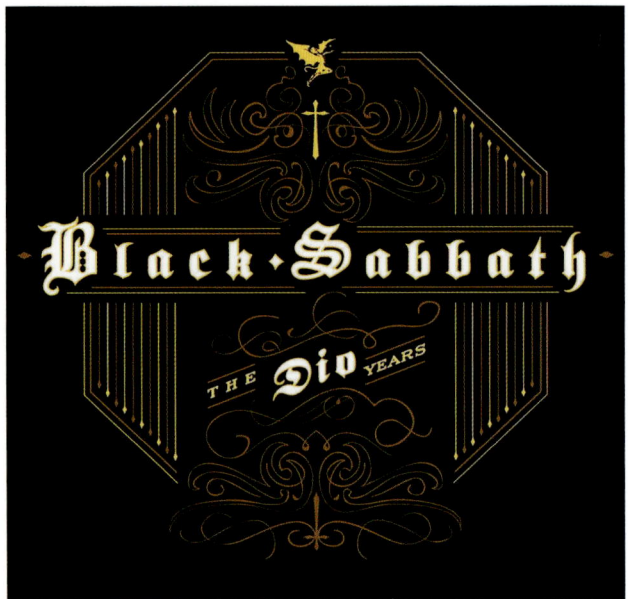

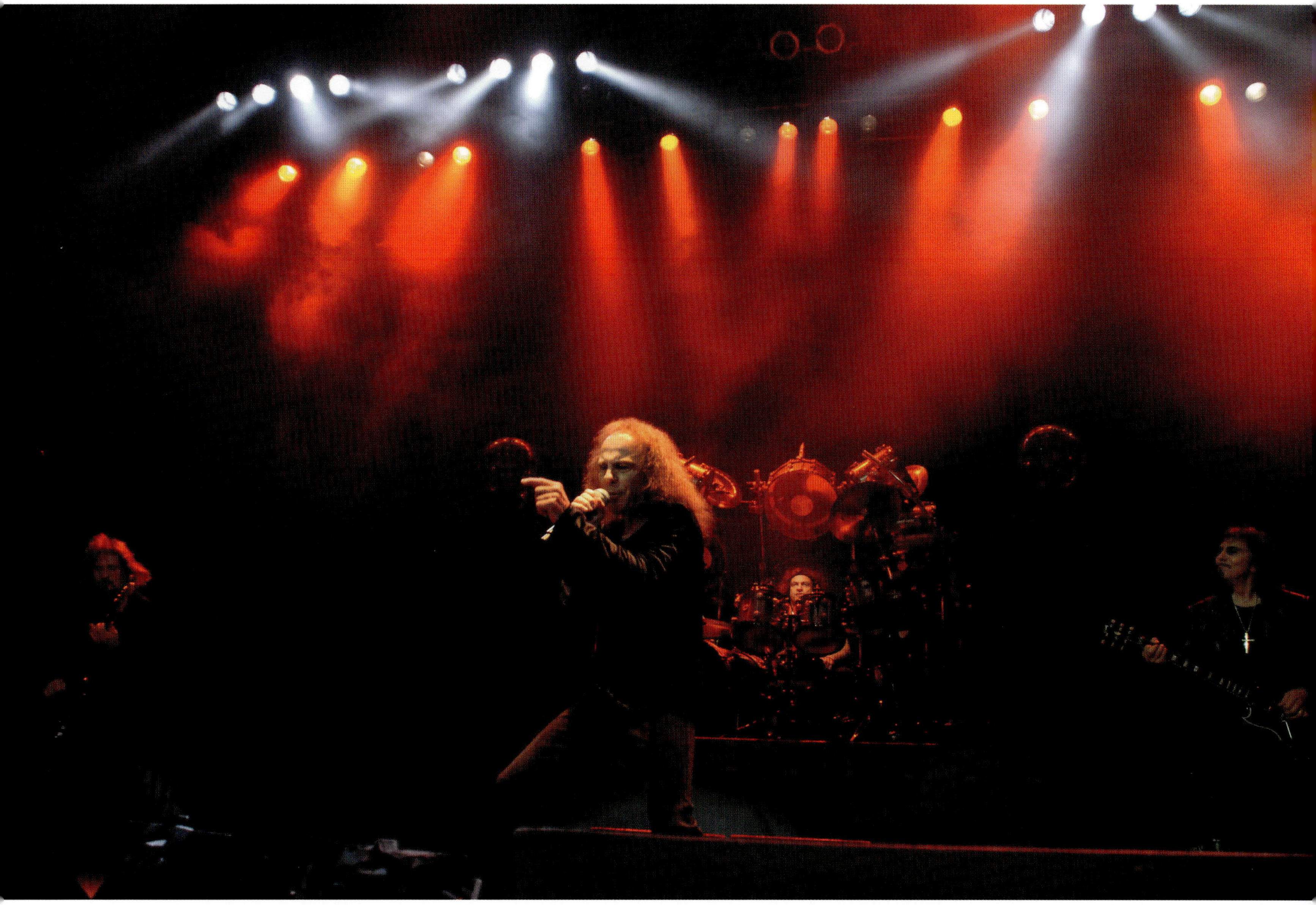

OPPOSITE: **Black Sabbath: The Dio Years** *is a 2007 compilation CD from when Ronnie James Dio fronted the band.*
ABOVE: *Heaven and Hell, fronted by Ronnie James Dio, playing at the House of Blues in Atlantic City, New Jersey, in August 2009.*

songs appeared: "The Devil Cried," "Shadow of the Wind," and "Ear in the Wall" made it clear that the Dio/Iommi songwriting partnership was firing once more on all cylinders.

Promoters queued up to book Heaven and Hell for live dates, and a tour was announced for March 2007, featuring high-profile support acts such as Down, Machine Head, and Megadeth. Although Ozzy had his own album out that year—*Black Rain*, a likable collection of songs—Sabbath fans' attention was largely focused on the long series of dates executed by Heaven and Hell, as the band continued to tour into 2008–2009.

A studio album, *The Devil You Know*, appeared in April 2009, and was followed by a four-month tour that took in European festival dates. The songs varied from upbeat

riffage ("Rock 'n' Roll Angel," "Breaking Into Heaven") to more somber, doom-laden tunes ("Atom and Evil," "Double the Pain"), while the slick arrangements of the songs revealed that the band was operating at full capacity. If you saw the band that year, you witnessed a magical spectacle, with Dio and the other musicians delivering a classic set that showed them to be at the peak of their powers.

Ozzy was busy, in the meantime, launching a lawsuit against Iommi, based on his claim that the Black Sabbath band name should be equally owned by the guitarist and himself. Iommi kept quiet on the matter, but it's known that a part of Ozzy's suit rested on his claim that his "signature lead vocals" were largely responsible for the band's success, and that Sabbath's profile had declined in the sixteen years during which Ozzy had not

been a member. He had a point, and the judge awarded in his favor.

Around this time, Ozzy dispensed with the services of his longtime guitarist, Zakk Wylde, who focused from that point on his band Black Label Society, and recruited a hotshot new axe-man in the form of Gus G. (Kostas Karamitroudis), who had become famous in the power-metal band Firewind. Ozzy's band also featured bassist Rob "Blasko" Nicholson, keyboard player Adam Wakeman, and drummer Tommy Clufetos.

"I got the call to play with Black Sabbath when I met Sharon Osbourne at a gig I was doing a few years ago," Wakeman explained, "and after I'd played with Sabbath for a while they asked me if I'd like to play in Ozzy's solo band as well. It seemed natural for me to play with those guys, because my dad [Rick Wakeman] had played keyboards and piano on *Sabbath Bloody Sabbath* back in 1973. They're all great people, and some of the guys there have been with them for a very long time, which is always a good sign."

It had been Nicholson's job to find a replacement for Wylde. "I was just flipping through some magazines," the bassist recalled, "and I saw some stuff that Gus had done. He'd played with Arch Enemy on the Ozzfest in 2005 that I was also on, and he went into the Ozzfest office and gave them a Firewind CD—so he put himself on the radar years ago."

Gus G. had attended the renowned music college Berklee, but dropped out after a few weeks. "I wanted to play in a rock band," he said, "rather than pay fuckin' twenty grand a year to be a college boy. I asked myself what good it was going to do me, when I didn't want to be a guitar teacher or a session guitarist who plays on commercials.

"I got an e-mail from Ozzy's management: it must have been someone who remembered me from the Ozzfest in 2005. They were like, 'Would you like to come down and do an audition?' At first I thought, 'What the fuck? Did Zakk lose an arm or something?' I thought I had nothing to lose, and I should definitely go down there and meet the man, jam with him and see what happens. I didn't really think I was gonna get the job. I flew to L.A. from my home town, Thessaloniki, and I did the audition and it went very well."

As Ozzy and his new band recorded a new album, Heaven and Hell was finishing its US tour. A live DVD, *Neon Nights*, was recorded on July 20, 2009, but all was not well behind the scenes: Dio was experiencing stomach

OPPOSITE: *The Devil You Know, released in 2009, is the only studio album from Heaven and Hell.* LEFT: *Heaven and Hell released* Neon Nights, *a live album recorded in 2009, after the death of Ronnie James Dio in 2010.* ABOVE: *Dio's memorial on May 30, 2010, at the Hall of Liberty in the Hollywood Hills.*

pains, which were diagnosed in November as stomach cancer. The great vocalist fought the disease for seven months before succumbing in May 2010.

Heaven and Hell played its final show at London's Victoria Park on July 24, 2010, as part of the High Voltage Festival, a new event

created by *Classic Rock* magazine. Glenn Hughes and Masterplan singer Jørn Lande, both friends of Dio's, stepped in to perform the vocals in tribute to him. At sixty-seven, he had died long before his time, and before Heaven and Hell could follow up on its excellent debut album. The rock world still mourns him.

I AM OZZY

In 2010, Ozzy published his autobiography, *I Am Ozzy*, a well-crafted and amusing run-through of as much of his life to date as he could recall. By now, his lawsuit against Iommi had been settled: a joint statement clarified that they had "amicably resolved their problems over the ownership of the Black Sabbath name, and court proceedings in New York have been discontinued. Both parties are glad to put this behind them and to cooperate together for the future and would like it to be known that the issue was never personal, it was always business."

When I asked him about the case in the summer of 2010, Ozzy explained, "It was just a thing that I had to do, because it was pointed out to me that band names like Deep Purple and Black Sabbath and Led Zeppelin are a brand name—like all kinds of things; wine, fucking beer, fucking clothes, logos—and I wanted my fair crack of the whip, so I had no other alternative but to do it. I spoke to Tony when I came back [from his recent tour]. Business and friendship are completely

LEFT: *Butler, Appice, and Iommi of Heaven and Hell perform a tribute to their deceased singer, Ronnie James Dio, in Victoria Park, London, on July 24, 2010. Jørn Lande fills in as their singer.*

different, and I love those guys—all of them."

In June of that year, Ozzy's new album, *Scream*, was released by Sony. The singer said of the record, "People say it's progressive, it's different; they say it's overproduced or they say they love it—y'know, I've never gone into a studio [thinking] I've had a great, successful career, I'm gonna do a shit album for once. Know what I mean? Every time I go in and do an album, I try to do a different album. There's a track on the album I really like called 'Life Won't Wait' with a different kind of a vibe—it's a really interesting sound, you know.

"Gus is wonderful," he continued. "If I hire a guy who's got a name, then I've got to deal with his fuckin' ego. I like to get people who are hungry for it, you know, [not like] some fucking Ritchie Blackmore or someone else who's known as a great guitarist. Every time I get a new guitar player, it's always tough. The one thing I always say is that nothing happened with Zakk. What happened was, it was time for me to get a permanent replacement, because Zakk didn't need me any more. Zakk's got Black Label Society and he's doing great. This band's been working great: we did a couple of gigs in Europe when I was just over there, and it was good fun."

LEFT: *Ozzy signing copies of his book,* I Am Ozzy, *at a signing at Borders in Las Vegas in February 2010.* **ABOVE:** Scream *is Ozzy's eleventh studio album, released in 2010.* **OPPOSITE:** *Ozzy's new guitarist for* Scream, *Gus G., playing with the band at the House of Blues in West Hollywood in June 2010.*

Of his autobiography, the singer explained, "What's a problem for me is my short-term memory. I don't know if it's my age or what, but I'll fucking go up and down stairs all day going 'What the fuck did I come up here for?' It's probably a combination of the [quad bike] accident and my age, I dunno. Without Chris Ayres, the guy who did the ghostwriting for me, I'd still be on fuckin' page one: I can't sit still for five minutes. Anyway, we got to the end and he said he had enough for another book, although I thought he was just winding me up. So probably that'll be called *I Am Still Ozzy*, or something."

"I don't drink, I don't smoke, I don't do drugs," he continued, when I asked about his personal pleasures. "All I can say is, I tried [drugs] when I was young and it nearly fucking . . . how I'm here, talking to you now, I really don't know. I don't think it's a good idea. I don't do it any more and I like [my life] much better without it. I used to think I couldn't enjoy making music if I wasn't stoned, but it doesn't work. Out of the question.

"The availability now is so fuckin' more than it used to be. For instance, I have a house in England near Beaconsfield, which is a picture-postcard fuckin' village, and one of the local bobbies was talking to me one day and he said, 'Every Friday and Saturday night, the kids we see, nine times out of ten they're carrying crack or some fuckin' thing.' It's scary. It's like the thing to do now. Cocaine, when I was younger, you had to know somebody who knew somebody who knew somebody. Now you can get it in the fuckin'

pub. . . . I don't think smoking too much fuckin' cannabis is gonna kill you, though, because you can't smoke as many cannabis cigarettes as you can regular cigarettes. You can have a go, but there'd be a lot of food being eaten."

In 2011, Ozzy's son Jack produced a documentary called *God Bless Ozzy Osbourne*. The film digs deeply, sometimes painfully so, into his past as a useless father—a side of the man that had only been alluded to before, most recently in his autobiography. The core of the film is not his history as a musician,

although obviously there was ample footage from his Black Sabbath and solo years; it's about the addictions that had plagued him for decades, rendering him incapable of giving his children the support they needed when they were young.

To the credit of both Jack and Ozzy, the film pulls no punches, with the older Osbourne offspring, Jessica and Louis, appearing visibly irritated as they recalled their dad's constant absences and worse, his intoxicated presence. Ozzy swerves these accusations to an extent, blaming his behavior—as some addicts tend to do—on the insidious nature of addiction itself, rather than taking full responsibility for it. As such, it's ever-so-slightly unsatisfying, especially at the film's end, when Ozzy is revealed to be five years clean and sober. The last few minutes, which imply that everything is going to be just fine, don't quite ring true, largely because the singer has spent virtually the entire film warning us that addiction is powerful and often returns to haunt its victims.

There's a lot of highly watchable stuff before we get to that point, though. The camera follows Ozzy as he returns to the suburban Birmingham house where he grew up, and into the bedroom he occupied as a kid: it's a pleasant place now, in stark contrast with the terrible desolation that surrounded it back in the 1950s. His recollections of the late Randy Rhoads are poignant, too, and while the 1990s are largely skipped over, the family's memories of the MTV series that made them stars are surprisingly candid. (It wasn't fun.)

OPPOSITE: *A promotional poster for Jack Osbourne's documentary of his father.* **ABOVE:** *Jack Osbourne at a screening of* God Bless Ozzy Osbourne *in Los Angeles in August 2011.*

Along the way, admirers such as Tommy Lee and Henry Rollins add mildly amusing contributions, but the central thrust is Ozzy's family and bandmates, as it should be. "You can't change what you've done, but you can change the way you're going to do things in the future," he says.

THE END OF THE BEGINNING OF THE END

In November 2011, promotional images bearing the numbers "11-11-11" appeared on Black Sabbath's social media pages. Sabbath's third reunion—or fourth, if you include Live Aid back in 1985—was about to occur, and when it did, it would be an occasion to remember. All four original members confirmed that live dates and an album produced by the veteran console-tweaker Rick Rubin were on their way. The record, to be titled *13*—to mark the number of albums Sabbath had released—was scheduled to appear in 2013.

The delight that many observers felt at Sabbath's return was diminished when

Iommi issued the dismal news in January 2012 that he was suffering from lymphoma, a cancer of the blood that appears in the lymphatic system. The following month, Bill Ward announced that he would not be taking part in the forthcoming album and tour for contractual reasons.

It got worse: on April 16, Ozzy posted a message to Facebook that read, "For the last year and a half I have been drinking and taking drugs. I was in a very dark place and was an asshole to the people I love most, my family. However, I am happy to say that I am now forty-four days sober. Just to set the record straight, Sharon and I are not divorcing. I'm just trying to be a better person. I would like to apologize to Sharon, my family, my friends,

and my bandmates for my insane behavior during this period . . . and my fans. God Bless, Ozzy." (This episode is documented in full in Sharon's 2013 book *Unbreakable*.)

Eventually, *13* was recorded with Rage Against the Machine drummer Brad Wilk taking Ward's place; Ozzy's touring drummer Tommy Clufetos stepped up to play the subsequent tour dates. Sabbath fans lined up for tickets to three re-re-reunion shows at Birmingham, Download, and Lollapalooza, each one featuring an excellent new song, "God Is Dead?," which was also released as a single. A second single, "End of the Beginning," was heard on May 15 in an episode of *CSI: Crime Scene Investigation* in which the band members themselves also appeared.

Sabbath toured for the rest of 2013, with dates in Australia and New Zealand—the

OPPOSITE: *The Black Sabbath reunion press conference on November 11, 2011, at the Whisky a Go Go in West Hollywood. Veteran console-tweaker Rick Rubin, stands between Ozzy and Tony.* **TOP:** *Sabbath performing on American TV drama CSI in March 2013.* **ABOVE:** *Actors Ted Danson (left) and Marc Vann watch Black Sabbath perform during their guest appearance.*

BLACK SABBATH

band's first shows there for forty years—and then North and South America, before more gigs in Europe. On June 10, *13* was released and instantly went to No. 1 in the UK and America, due largely to the fact that the music was almost uniformly fantastic—the most charismatic recordings that Sabbath had created in decades. High points include "God Is Dead?," "End of the Beginning," and the utterly convincing "Zeitgeist," the best Sabbath ballad in years.

Promoting the album, Iommi—who was successfully fighting cancer with a series of intermittent treatments between tour legs—looked back at his early career with an interview with the author of this book. Asked if he considered himself responsible for the invention of heavy metal, he replied, "I suppose I was the first to come up with that style, and tune down. The things I went through in the early days to try and convince everybody—it was always, 'You can't do this, you can't do that, that's not right.' But I just took no notice. So heavy metal obviously didn't exist before that, or I wouldn't have had those problems. Everybody always says I was the first, and I suppose I think that too."

Asked how he had managed to avoid the addiction issues that had plagued his former colleague Bill Ward, among others, the guitarist explained, "I got hooked on cocaine for a while in the late '70s, but I didn't need treatment—I've always sorted it out myself. I did have my moments with alcohol, too. I used to get quite sloshed sometimes, but the others carried on every night, more and more. I felt that somebody had to be in control."

Physically, Iommi was enduring various problems relating to his guitar playing—understandable, given his lengthy career onstage. "I have to warm up a lot these days, because I've got this problem with my thumb—the cartilage has gone, so it's just bone on bone. The doctors have suggested an operation to fuse the two joints together and make it stiff, which I'm really worried about. Apart from that, there's not a lot they can do—I have to take painkillers. I did have shots in my hand a few times, but you can only do those for so long.

"Also, I broke a tendon in the same arm when I was lifting weights, and it's still broken—and I broke three tendons in that arm a few years ago, just from wear and tear. I had them repaired, which took a while to heal, but on this last tour—at the last New York

OPPOSITE: *Sabbath's nineteenth studio album, 13, was released in 2013. The album featured Ozzy, Iommi, and Butler; Ward decided not to participate for contractual reasons.*
LEFT: *Sabbath accepting a Grammy Award in 2014 for Best Metal Performance for the song "God Is Dead?"*
BELOW: *Butler (left) and Tommy Clufetos (right) playing at Mohegan Sun Casino in Connecticut during the 13 tour in August 2013.*

show—I was doing some exercise, and bang! One of them went in my bicep. I haven't got time to get it repaired. It's really annoying, because these things all happen to the same arm—first I cut the fingertips off, and then I had carpal tunnel problems, and now all the tendons are going. I'm falling to bits, basically!"

Asked if he realized that there was no other metal guitar player of his age who was still recording and touring at stadium level, he mused, "Well, I do love going onstage. For me, it's the traveling that I can't stand—getting there and back. I don't think about retiring, though. I've been asked about it since I was twenty-five years old, and the answer is, I'll keep doing it until I can't do it any more. Or until people don't want to hear it."

Iommi remained careful not to draw too much inspiration from elsewhere. "I try not to listen to [other music] while I'm writing, because it can creep into your music if you're not careful. I lock myself away in my own world. Touch wood, ideas still come along very well: I record my riffs into a little machine and when it's full I listen to them. I sit in bed and riffs come to me—and if I can get an idea down on tape, even with a crap sound, it's okay, as long as you don't rub it off accidentally.

"My daughter's in a band," he concluded, "and whatever I tell her goes in one ear and

LEFT: *Ozzy and Iommi playing at Mohegan Sun Casino in Connecticut during the 13 tour in August 2013.*

out the other. If you really love it, you've got to stick with it. We've all heard people tell us, 'You're playing the wrong stuff,' and 'Don't play that, play this,' but if you can just do what you believe in, eventually it'll come through."

Butler, too, gave me an illuminating interview around this time. "What led to Heaven and Hell in the first place was Tony and I wanting to go out on tour with our two solo bands," he explained, "but the company just wouldn't put the money up!" The end result of the Heaven and Hell tours, though, was that they improved him as a player. "I'm more confident about trying new things onstage—I used to hold back in case something didn't come off. I used to come up with new ways of playing a bass part when I was warming up, and then back out of trying it onstage! But this time I just go for it and if it doesn't work, it doesn't work. A few things have gone disastrously for me, which sounded great when I was on my own and don't work with the band—some of the stuff just doesn't fit. It's okay, though: I didn't realize how good the *Dehumanizer* record was until I went back and listened to it recently. Those songs have been given a new lease of life now that they're being played by this band.

Asked about his extravagant performance style, Butler explained, "I used to really *whomp* the bass strings, but I've taught myself to back off a bit. I still hit them extremely hard. I've no idea where I got that from, it's my natural style. I do get excited playing live: when I'm rehearsing I don't hit the strings anywhere near as hard as that, which gives

the soundman headaches. It's fun to play that way, particularly in songs like 'Voodoo' and 'Heaven and Hell,' where there's always room to throw a few things in. But with the old songs, I tend to stick to what I did on the records, even down to the fills—because there have been so many cover versions over the years that people like to hear the originals. If you play a song differently, you get all these bloody emails from people saying, 'You didn't play it properly!' People study the songs and say, 'Why did you put that note in there?'"

LOOKING BACK

When I spoke to Ozzy around the same time, he explained that he had some ambitions left to achieve—namely a collaboration with a certain modern pop icon. "Lady Gaga is very, very interesting," he said. "I would be up for that. But if I did something like that, my girls would fucking kill me: they'd be like, 'Why don't you do a song with us?' If the song was right, of course [I'd do it]. You know what I like about her? She's fuckin' interesting. She looks a bit special: that's what the music business should be about.

"I'd also love to do a duet with Paul McCartney: if he phoned right now, I'd drop everything and be on the next plane. My son Jack is doing a documentary about me and my life, and he said, 'What about getting Paul McCartney?' and I said, 'No, he wouldn't

OPPOSITE: *Ozzy Osbourne, photographed around 2014.*

fucking be interviewed about me,' and he said, 'I've asked him, and he said he would,' and I was like, 'What?' I think the man's fucking great. When you see him play live, you go, 'Fucking hell!'"

After so many years in the music business, I was curious to see if Ozzy had any advice for young bands who might be attempting to break into the music industry. "Nowadays? Fuckin' hell!" he retorted. "The other day, I was informed that new bands who've just signed with their record companies have to give away part of their publishing, part of their gig money, part of their concessions, whatever . . . what the fuck is going on? I wouldn't like to be one of the bands of today. It's fuckin' disgusting the way they treat the bands.

"One thing I can really say I'm proud of is that Black Sabbath were four guys from Aston, Birmingham—which is not that big— who had a dream that came true, bigger than we ever expected. That's never gonna happen again, with today's market. You've got to be a computer fuckin' expert now as well. It's changed so much. Someone can be the biggest thing in the world, and then the next month you go, 'What happened to them?' Record sales are no more—they aren't selling records that much any more, because of this downloading thing.

"You know what? When we were kids and we wanted to be successful, we didn't know what the fuck we were signing. We didn't know anything about publishing companies or whatever. Now you can go onto your computer and you can fuckin' find out what to go for. You can open your laptop and find out what a manager's average fuckin' percentage is. But if you make it, there's big money to be made—and the moment big money happens, people get weird. I said to Bill Ward once, 'Regardless of the fact that we got ripped off [by management], all our lifestyles improved about 15,000 times higher than they had been.' Our lives did get a lot better. We had cars, we had houses, we could go and have a pint when we wanted, and we could buy our own packet of cigarettes, rather than just one between the four of us."

Wise words. Have Black Sabbath made a positive impact on the world? I'd say so, and if you've read this far, presumably you do, too. It's a long way from the satanic panic of the '80s, when Sabbath and their ilk were viewed as a negative influence on the youth of the day. Were they ever really a threat? Of course not.

In fact, Black Sabbath's collective behavior as the band's career wound up in 2017 was anything but threatening. It was, if anything, rather dignified. Although a follow-up album to *13* was considered, and even mentioned in press interviews, Ozzy and crew made it clear in 2016 that the writing was on the wall for Sabbath, announcing a farewell world tour

PREVIOUS SPREAD AND OPPOSITE: *Sabbath playing at New York's Madison Square Garden during* **The End** *tour on February 25, 2016.*

called *The End*. This, apparently, really was it, for the band that had said farewell at least twice before.

The final tour ran from January 2016 to February the following year, taking in a final Download festival performance in June. As the crowds suffered under the wettest weather in the festival's history, the band powered through a classic set, apparently at the peak of their powers. It was especially pleasing when Iommi announced in August that his cancer was in remission.

The triumphant final flight of Black Sabbath was marred only by the sad news of long-time collaborator Geoff Nicholls' death in January 2017. *The End* tour finally concluded on February 4 with a hometown gig at Birmingham's Genting Arena. As the band finished their set, rumors began to

fly about their next move. Even an official announcement of their breakup on February 7 didn't quell the public enthusiasm for more Sabbath activity, helped along by Iommi's admission that one-off gigs and recordings might take place in the future.

Meanwhile, Ozzy wasted no time in preparing for renewed solo activity by re-recruiting guitarist Zakk Wylde for plans still to be announced. There's more music to come from the members of Sabbath, make no mistake.

The title of this book is a question as much as a statement, and the answer to the question, "What evil lurks?"—at least within the minds of Ozzy, Iommi, Butler, Ward, Dio, and the other great characters that populate the story—is "None." But there is genius in abundance, and that is to be celebrated.

BLACK SABBATH LINE-UPS

1969–1979
Ozzy Osbourne (vocals)
Tony Iommi (guitar)
Geezer Butler (bass)
Bill Ward (drums)

1979
Ronnie James Dio (vocals)
Tony Iommi (guitar)
Geezer Butler (bass)
Bill Ward (drums)

1979–1982
Ronnie James Dio (vocals)
Tony Iommi (guitar)
Geezer Butler (bass)
Vinny Appice (drums)

1982–1984
Ian Gillan (vocals)
Tony Iommi (guitar)
Geezer Butler (bass)
Bill Ward (drums)

1985–1986
Glenn Hughes (vocals)
Tony Iommi (guitar)
Eric Spitz (bass)
Eric Singer (drums)

1987–1988
Tony Martin (vocals)
Tony Iommi (guitar)
Eric Spitz (bass)
Eric Singer (drums)

1988–1989
Tony Martin (vocals)
Tony Iommi (guitar)
Cozy Powell (drums)

1990
Tony Martin (vocals)
Tony Iommi (guitar)
Neil Murray (bass)
Cozy Powell (drums)

1991–1993
Ronnie James Dio (vocals)
Tony Iommi (guitar)
Geezer Butler (bass)
Vinny Appice (drums)

1994–1995
Tony Martin (vocals)
Tony Iommi (guitar)
Neil Murray (bass)
Cozy Powell (drums)

1997–2017
Ozzy Osbourne (vocals)
Tony Iommi (guitar)
Geezer Butler (bass)
Bill Ward (drums)

**Additional touring or
recording musicians**

Vocals
Dave Walker (1977–1978)
Ron Keel (1984)
David Donato (1984–1985)
Ray Gillen (1986–1987)

Bass
Craig Gruber (1979)
Bob Daisley (1987)
Laurence Cottle (1988–1989)

Drums
Terry Chimes (1987)
Jo Burt (1987)
Bobby Rondinelli (1993–1994,
   1995)
Mike Bordin (1997)
Brad Wilk (2012–2013)
Tommy Clufetos (2013–2016)

Keyboards
Bev Bevan (1983–1984, 1987)
Geoff Nicholls (1986–2004)

BLACK SABBATH DISCOGRAPHY

Singles

"Evil Woman"
Fontana, 1970 (UK —, US —)

"Paranoid"
Vertigo, 1970 (UK #4, US —)

"Never Say Die"
Vertigo, 1978 (UK #21, US —)

"Hard Road"
Vertigo, 1978 (UK #33, US —)

"Neon Knights"
Vertigo, 1980 (UK #22, US —)

"Die Young"
Vertigo, 1980 (UK #41, US —)

"Mob Rules"
Vertigo, 1981 (UK #46, US —)

"Turn Up the Night"
Vertigo, 1982 (UK #37, US 24)

"Voodoo"
Vertigo, 1982 (UK —, US #46)

"Headless Cross"
IRS, 1989 (UK #62, US —)

"TV Crimes"
IRS, 1992 (UK #33, US —)

"The Hand That Rocks the
   Cradle"
IRS, 1994 (UK —, US —)

"Psycho Man"
Epic, 1998 (UK —, US #3)

"Selling My Soul"
Epic, 1999 (UK —, US #17)

"The Devil Cried"
Rhino, 2007 (UK —, US #38)

"God Is Dead?"
Warners, 2013 (UK #145, US #7)

"End of the Beginning"
Warners, 2013 (UK —, US #38)

"Loner"
Warners, 2013 (UK —, US —)

"Loner (Live)"
Warners, 2013 (UK —, US —)

"Age of Reason"
Warners, 2013 (UK —, US —)

Albums

Black Sabbath
Vertigo, 1970 (UK #8, US #23)

Paranoid
Vertigo, 1970 (UK #1, US #12)

Master of Reality
Vertigo, 1971 (UK #5, US #8)

Volume 4
Vertigo, 1972 (UK #8, US #13)

Sabbath Bloody Sabbath
Vertigo, 1973 (UK #4, US #11)

Sabotage
NEMS, 1975 (UK #7, US #28)

We Sold Our Soul for Rock 'n' Roll
NEMS, 1975 (UK #35, US #48)

Technical Ecstasy
Vertigo, 1976 (UK #13, US #51)

Never Say Die!
Vertigo, 1978 (UK #12, US #69)

Heaven and Hell
Vertigo, 1980 (UK #9, US #28)

Live at Last
NEMS, 1980 (UK #5, US—)

Mob Rules
Mercury, 1981 (UK #12, US #29)

Live Evil
Vertigo, 1982 (UK #13, US #37)

Born Again
Vertigo, 1983 (UK #4, US #39)

Seventh Star
Vertigo, 1986 (UK #27, US #78)

The Eternal Idol
Vertigo, 1987 (UK #66, US #168)

Headless Cross
IRS, 1989 (UK #31, US #115)

Tyr
IRS, 1990 (UK #24, US —)

Dehumanizer
IRS, 1992 (UK #28, US #44)

Cross Purposes
IRS, 1994 (UK #41, US #122)

Cross Purposes Live
IRS, 1994 (UK —, US —)

Forbidden
IRS, 1995 (UK #71, US —)

The Sabbath Stones
IRS, 1996 (UK —, US —)

Reunion
Epic, 1998 (UK #41, US #11)

The Best of Black Sabbath
Metal-Is, 2000 (UK #24, US —)

Past Lives
Sanctuary, 2002 (UK —, US #114)

Black Box: Black Sabbath 1970–1978
Rhino, 2004 (UK —, US —)

Greatest Hits 1970–1978
Rhino, 2006 (UK —, US #96)

Black Sabbath: The Dio Years
Rhino, 2007 (UK #151, US #54)

Live at Hammersmith Odeon
Rhino, 2007 (UK —, US —)

The Rules of Hell
Rhino, 2008 (UK —, US —)

Greatest Hits
Universal, 2009 (UK #19, US —)

Iron Man: The Best of Black Sabbath
Universal, 2012 (UK #12, US —)

13
Vertigo, 2013 (UK #1, US #1)

Live . . . Gathered in Their Masses
Vertigo, 2013 (UK —, US —)

Ozzy Osbourne Singles

"Crazy Train"
Jet, 1980 (UK #49, US —)

"Mr Crowley"
Jet, 1980 (UK #46, US —)

"Bark at the Moon"
Epic, 1983 (UK #21, US —)

"So Tired"
Epic, 1984 (UK #20, US —)

"Shot in the Dark"
Epic, 1986 (UK #20, US #68)

"The Ultimate Sin / Lightning
    Strikes"
Epic, 1986 (UK #72, US —)

"No More Tears"
Epic, 1991 (UK #32, US #71)

"Mama I'm Coming Home"
Epic, 1992 (UK #46, US #28)

"Perry Mason"
Epic, 1995 (UK #23, US —)

"I Just Want You"
Epic, 1996 (UK #43, US —)

"Dreamer"
Epic, 2002 (UK #18, US —)

"Changes" (with Kelly Osbourne)
Sanctuary, 2003 (UK #1, US —)

Ozzy Osbourne Albums
Blizzard of Ozz
Jet, 1980 (UK #7, US #21)

Diary of a Madman
Jet, 1981 (UK #14, US #16)

Speak of the Devil
Jet, 1982 (UK #21, US #14)

Bark at the Moon
Epic, 1983 (UK #24, US #19)

The Ultimate Sin
Epic, 1986 (UK #8, US #6)

Tribute
Epic, 1987 (UK #13, US #6)

No Rest for the Wicked
Epic, 1988 (UK #23, US #13)

Just Say Ozzy
Epic, 1990 (UK #69, US #58)

No More Tears
Epic, 1991 (UK #17, US #7)

Ozzmosis
Epic, 1995 (UK #22, US #4)

The Ozzman Cometh
Epic, 1997 (UK #68, US #13)

Down to Earth
Epic, 2001 (UK #19, US #4)

The Essential Ozzy Osbourne
Epic, 2003 (UK #21, US #81)

Prince of Darkness
Sanctuary, 2005 (UK —, US #36)

Under Cover
Sanctuary, 2005 (UK —, US #134)

Black Rain
Epic, 2007 (UK #8, US #3)

Scream
Epic, 2010 (UK #12, US #4)

Tony Iommi Albums
Iommi
Divine, 2000 (UK —, US #129)

The 1996 Dep Sessions
Mayan, 2004 (UK —, US —)

Fused
Sanctuary, 2005 (UK —, US —)

Geezer Butler Albums
Plastic Planet
Raw Power, 1995 (UK —, US —)

Black Science
Sum, 1997 (UK —, US —)

Ohmwork
Mayan, 2005 (UK —, US —)

Bill Ward Albums
Ward One: Along the Way
Chameleon, 1990 (UK —, US —)

When the Bough Breaks
Cleopatra, 1997 (UK —, US —)

Heaven and Hell Albums
Live from Radio City Music Hall
Rhino, 2007 (UK —, US —)

The Devil You Know
Rhino, 2009 (UK #21, US #8)

*Neon Nights: 30 Years of Heaven
    and Hell . . .*
Eagle Rock, 2010 (UK —, US —)

Please note that Black Sabbath's albums
have been reissued on several occasions,
notably by the Sanctuary imprint Castle,
in a variety of formats (CD, enhanced CD,
miniature LP replica, you name it).

PHOTOGRAPHY CREDITS

INDEX

ACKNOWLEDGMENTS

Emma, Alice, Tom, Robin and Kate, Dad, John and Jen, Chris Akin, Scott Bartlett, Max and Gloria Cavalera, Joe Daly, Jeannine Dillon, Helen Donlon, John Doran, Mark Eglinton, David Ellefson, Marty Friedman, Robb Flynn, Lisa Gallagher, Matthew Hamilton, Glenn Hughes, Joseph Huston, Bill Irwin, Borivoj Krgin, John Mayall, Bob Nalbandian, Suzanne Penley, Martin Popoff, Ralph Santolla, Tom Seabrook, Tony Spiess, Wes Stanton, David Vincent, Mick Wall, Woody Woodmansey, the editorial and marketing teams at Hal Leonard, the staff of Blaze Publishing, the writers at *Bass Guitar Magazine*, and the families Alderman, Arnold, Barnes, Bhardwaj, Boot-Handford, Bowles, Cadette, Carr, Desire, Edwards, Ellis, Fraser, Freed, Harper, Harrington, Herbert-Jones, Hogben, Homes, Jolliffe, Knight, Lamond, Lamont, Legerton, Leim, Mathieson Spires, Maynard, Mendonça, Metcalfe, Miles, Parr, Pelgrift, Sendall, Skeens, Storey, Turner, Williams, and Woollard, the many fine writers who have reviewed my books in recent years, and of course the visitors to joelmciver.co.uk, facebook.com/joelmciver, and @joelmciver.

ABOUT THE AUTHOR

JOEL McIVER is the best-selling author of thirty books on rock music and contributes to many magazines and newspapers. He is often seen and heard on BBC and commercial TV and radio and lives near London, England.